Hadley in the Civil War

ERIC N. FREEMAN

Hadley in the Civil War

WHITE RIVER PRESS
Amherst, Massachusetts

Privately published 1992. Revised and expanded 2009.

A PUBLICATION OF HADLEY'S 350TH CELEBRATION

White River Press
P.O. Box 3561
Amherst, MA 01004
www.whiteriverpress.com

Printed in the United States of America

ISBN: 978-1-935052-23-4

Front cover photo Marker for Frederick S. Russell (1834-1862).
North Hadley Cemetery. Photo taken by James A. Freeman
Layout and cover design by Patricia Nobre

Library of Congress Cataloging-in-Publication Data

Freeman, Eric N. (Eric Noble), 1973-
Hadley in the Civil War / Eric N. Freeman.
p. cm.

"Privately published 1992. Revised and expanded 2009"--T.p. verso.

Includes bibliographical references.
ISBN 978-1-935052-23-4 (pbk.)
1. Hadley (Mass. : Town)--History--19th century. 2. Hadley
(Mass. : Town)--History, Military--19th century. 3. Hadley (Mass.
: Town)--Social life and customs--19th century. 4. Soldiers--
Massachusetts--Hadley (Town)--Biography. 5. Hadley (Mass.
: Town)--Biography. 6. Massachusetts--History--Civil War,
1861-1865--Social aspects. 7. Massachusetts--History--Civil
War, 1861-1865--Influence. 8. United States--History--Civil War,
1861-1865--Social aspects. 9. United States--History--Civil War,
1861-1865--Influence. I. Title.

F74.H1F74 2010
974.4'2304--dc22
                                           2009052194

Contents

New Preface to the 350th Anniversary Reprint _____ i
Original Dedication _____ iii
Preface _____ v

Chapter One: The Typical Rural Town: 1860 _____ 1
Chapter Two: Many Calls to Arms _____ 7
Chapter Three: Who Answered the Calls? _____ 19
Chapter Four: Why Did Enthusiasm Die? _____ 23
Chapter Five: Real People _____ 29
    A. Joseph Hooker _____ 29
    B. H. Clement Russell _____ 32
    C. John Dunbar and *Dances With Wolves* _____ 34
Chapter Six: Hadley, Post War _____ 37

Appendices _____ 41
    Hadley Residents Born Outside Massachusetts ____ 42
    Casualties _____ 43
    Sources and Symbols _____ 44
    Name, Age, Occupation, Marital Status, Origin,
    Race of Men Credited to Hadley _____ 45
    Additional Sources _____ 57
    Abbreviations for Military Units _____ 60
    Abbreviations for Service Histories _____ 60
    Service History of Hadley Men _____ 61

Endnotes _____ 79

New Preface to the
350th Anniversary Reprint

The following essay about Hadley soldiers in the Civil War was originally submitted to the History faculty of Deerfield Academy in 1991. Although it began as a routine school assignment, it soon became a personal mission. How, I wondered, could boys little older than me have volunteered for such horror? What did they do before becoming Union soldiers? Why did they not avoid the inevitable sickness, exhaustion, imprisonment, pain and death that any war necessitates? They lived in a world that often seems remote today, one of group loyalty and family pride, all governed by a sense of duty. Research about their identities, their daily lives and their military careers helped me to reanimate them and finally give them the dignity they earned. My discoveries brought me closer to them and still move me with sadness and admiration.

Although the facts remain unchanged, four small additions appear. The wording of various sentences has, I hope, improved. Also, there are now updates to the historical bibliography. Third, you will find contemporary illustrations of the Civil War from widely-read popular magazines like *Harper's Weekly*. These images brought into ordinary homes spectacular scenes of rebel butchery, abused slaves, noble Union officers and epic battles as well as wretched prisoners, mutilated veterans and shabby burials. Alternately sensational and sentimental, the engravings molded opinion more graphically than sermons or speeches and no doubt prodded many men to volunteer.

Finally, I have also amplified my suggestion that Reverend John Brown (1804-1857) and his son John Brown Dunbar (1843-1914) of Hadley were models for John Dunbar, the hero of Michael Blake's *Dances With Wolves*. The father was a prominent missionary to Native Americans and wrote extensive reports about their customs. His son grew up with Pawnees, returned to Hadley so he could attend Hopkins Academy and, after graduation, walk the five miles to Amherst College. He served in two Union regiments, then became a professor of Classics and librarian at Washburn University, Topeka, Kansas. Dunbar wrote authoritatively about the Pawnees with a sympathy not usually found in the later nineteenth century. True, he did not abandon white society, as does Blake's character, and he married a white woman, not the kidnapped and acculturated Stands With a Fist. Still, his atypical closeness to Native Americans and his vivid narratives certainly make him a possible model for Blake's compassionate veteran. When Mr. Blake kindly invited me to meet him in Cambridge, he courteously did not deny my premise.

I might add that this essay's reception surprised me and may give courage to other authors. I assumed my complete list of Hadley soldiers and their service histories would be useful. Instead of thanks from scholars, however, newspapers, television programs and historical groups from across the country sought me out for interviews about John Dunbar. My fifteen minutes of fame reminded me how little we control the outcome of our actions. May all of us appreciate these Hadley men who could not have suspected the great results their sacrifices would achieve for our entire nation.

Editorial note to the 350th edition: Since the original writing of this essay in 1991, scholarship on the Civil War has flourished. Anyone who would like to read further in the history of Massachusetts before, during and after the war may wish to consult Drew Gilpin Faust, *This Republic of Suffering: Death and the American Civil War* (New York: Vintage, 2009); Martin Griffin, *Ashes of the Mind: War and Memory in Northern Literature, 1865-1900* (Amherst: University of Massachusetts Press, 2009); Paul Alan Cimbala and Randall M. Miller, eds., *Union Soldiers and the Northern Home Front: Wartime Experiences, Postwar Adjustments* (Bronx: Fordham University Press, 2002); and Judith Giesberg, *Army at Home: Women and the Civil War on the Northern Home Front* (Chapel Hill: University of North Carolina Press, 2009). Some additional titles of interest have been inserted into the original work's endnotes, where relevant.

Original Dedication

To say the least, when I started this project, I felt overwhelmed. Each of the 233 Hadley soldiers who served during the terrible war of 1861-1865 had his personal history and I didn't know where to start. Unlike many New England towns such as Deerfield, we do not have a monument to a boy in blue who could look down from his timeless pedestal and silently encourage me. Except for the memorial boulder in front of General Joseph Hooker's home site on the West Street common, there is no obvious center for Civil War studies. A house in Easthampton reputedly had a basement tunnel so slaves on the Underground Railroad might slip secretly away, but even that building is now torn down.[1] I began my task by flipping through secondary sources, none of which shed much light on my topic. Sylvester Judd's standard *History of Hadley* was unfinished when he died in 1860. A man who had begun a new account of our past wrote me that he had not reached the mid-nineteenth century and thus could not help me.[2] Walter H. Hebert's *Fighting Joe Hooker* gives a full biography of the famous general, but spends only a few pages on the pre-war town. The massive lists in the nine-volume *Massachusetts Soldiers, Sailors, and Marines in the Civil War* and the earlier two-volume *Record of the Massachusetts Volunteers* did not make the men come alive in my imagination.

Luckily, I then phoned Ms. Dorothy Russell, Vice-President of the Hadley Historical Society. She pointed me in the right direction, opening the Historical Room in Goodwin Memorial Library so I could copy names from the town's list of volunteers, uncovering valuable handwritten documents from the vault of Town Hall and lending me the personal memoir of her grandfather, Clement H. Russell, who had served in company F, 37th regiment, Massachusetts Volunteer Infantry. Many times, she recalled, he would let her touch the scar on his head that he received at the Battle of the Wilderness. Her invaluable help inspired me during many hours of discovery. More important, she demonstrated that the past never disappears. It may hide for a while, but we should always try to recover it. This paper and charts are a small return that I now give her in return for her time and encouragement. Thank you, Ms. Russell. I hope you enjoy the information.

Preface

There are popular tales about community that parents tell their kids before they go bed. I recall the one about the country mouse going to visit his friend in the city, hating it, and then, oddly, having his friend fall in love with the country. The glamorous advertisements in L.L. Bean catalogues picture fashion-conscious urban folks in their comfortable "country clothes." But how many people really appreciate the advantages of living in a small village? I do. These little towns encourage a comfortable familiarity. One is acquainted with most residents or at least has heard of them. Our school system, the second smallest in Massachusetts, allows everyone to know everyone.

I had the pleasure of spending seven years in these schools. While attending the Joseph P. Hooker elementary school, I saw the boulder on the West Street common that marked the site of Parson Russell's house. There two judges who signed the order to execute King Charles I of England hid in a secret room during the 1660s. One, William Goffe, became known as "The Angel of Hadley" because he supposedly emerged from concealment to rescue townspeople from an attack by Native Americans in 1675. Still, the seventeenth century seemed so remote. Then in fourth grade my class visited Hooker's birthplace further north on the common. Now called the Byron home, my friend lived there with his mother, the school nurse. Electricity flowed in the air when my teacher Mrs. Mary Lou Cutter described the famous leader's involvement in the Civil War. The house was no longer ordinary. Hearing that the celebrity general who appears on the town seal and had given his name to my grade school was once there made me curious about this neglected part of my town's past. Were the other young men who lived in the village before me as unusual as he? Did their going off to war affect history?

While watching Ken Burn's *Civil War* series, I heard the narrator describe how Hooker blundered at Chancellorsville; he delayed, perhaps because part of a porch had fallen on his head, and cost the Union a much needed victory.[3] At first, I thought my ears had deceived me. No, this couldn't possibly be the same Hooker that I remembered from fourth grade. Not the proud, handsome general who was Lincoln's close friend and notable commander. It was almost like the heavens opened up and a voice said, "Eric, here is your term paper topic. Find out the truth about all these men." Deciding to set Hooker among other Hadley soldiers, I gathered facts in order to describe the 233 men who also fought in the Union army. In the parlance of their day, "they went to see the elephant," to have the fullest encounter with ultimate sights and totally unfamiliar sensations. Thus I came to ponder the Civil War experience of Hadley men - boys, really - from rural western Massachusetts. They traveled far from home and became immersed in worlds that they had scarcely imagined. The town's sons volunteered for various reasons, served in a variety of regiments, including the famous black 54th, and had different adventures. Some came home and, as in all wars, some did not. This paper honors all who participated.

Chapter One

The Typical Rural Town: 1860

In 1860, Hadley resembled many other villages in the Connecticut valley. Sandwiched between the larger communities of Sunderland to the north, Amherst College to the east and Northampton to the west, its homes and farms lay close to fields and two colleges, Amherst for men and Mount Holyoke Female Seminary for women. Most of the 2,230 residents farmed or made brooms.[4] Children who completed their primary years could attend the one high school, Hopkins Academy. Three churches, two in the center of town, the other in North Hadley, brought worshippers together for Sunday morning services and frequent festivals. There was a fire station and a grist mill, a ferry and stables. Barns to hold hay and tobacco stood picturesquely in fields, adding to its quaint, industrious New England look. Veterans of the War of 1812 grew old in this tranquil place. Probably few of the vigorous young men who helped Hadley prosper ever dreamed that soon their services would be needed in a great war.

Daily chores kept people busy. Hadley's broom mills were nationally famous as a center for manufacturing high quality brooms. From across the country, orders poured in and local shops hummed to ship them out. The broom business provided a perfect opportunity for residents both to farm and make brooms.

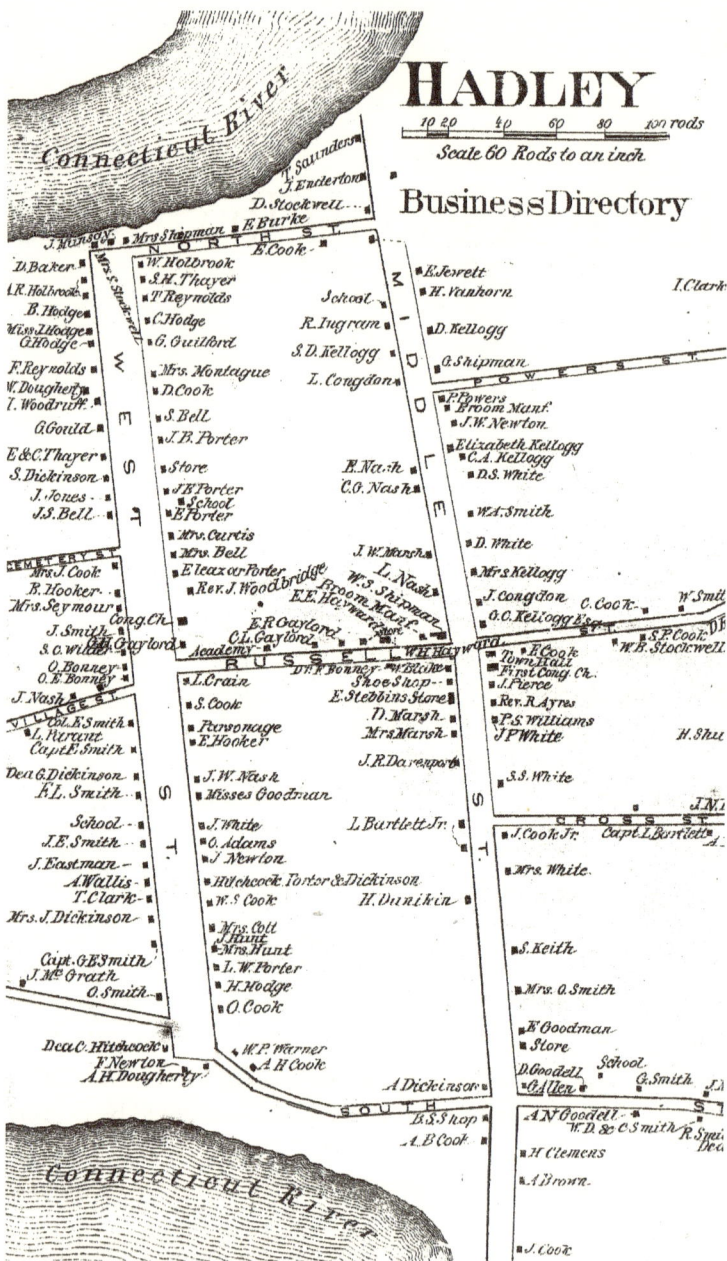

Figure 1: Hadley in 1860.
County Atlas of Hampshire. Massachusetts. from Actual Surveys by and under the Direction of F. W. Beers (New York: F. W. Beers, 1860).

During the spring, farmers would plant a special type of corn which produced the husks that served as the bristles on the broom. When fall came, they would gather these stiff, husked stalks. During winter, while fields were covered with snow, the farmers took their husks and made brooms until the process started over again.[5] Besides brooming, Hadley depended on its fertile soil to grow a variety of crops. Then, as now, corn and hay, apples and tobacco grew easily. When officials in Boston were debating the site for the new agricultural college (to be founded in 1863, and later called the University of Massachusetts), a loyal son of Hadley advertised his town's advantages by spotlighting "as great a variety of soils as can be found ... living springs, as pure and cool as ever bubbled from the heart of mother earth ... pure air."[6] Using the railroad, farmers would ship crops from these fertile fields to Boston and other cities.

The tobacco grown in Hadley was not used for chewing or smoking; instead it was rolled to form the outer leaf on cigars. Like brooms, the cigar tobacco was in high demand in northern states. Because Hadley had some of the most fertile soil in the state, its farmers could make a living by supplying the leaves to cigar factories. Newspaper accounts often told how much money various farmers made from their fields. An article quoted from the New York *Tribune* rightly claimed, "People have gone tobacco crazy" because they could make such big profits.[7] Large operators like Thaddeus Smith (who raised twenty-four tons on twenty-one acres[8]), E. P. Hibbard and L. N. Granger (who both raised nineteen tons on twenty-two acres) must have inspired smaller entrepreneurs like Benjamin Hooker, a relation of the general, who averaged 2444 pounds on each of his five acres, selling it for about $.50 per pound.[9]

But Hadley wasn't just a farm town. Many artisans and professionals made their homes here. Painters, mechanics, teamsters, blacksmiths, saddlers, wheelwrights, brass finishers, wire makers, butchers, teachers, coopers, lumbermen, potters, clerks, sailors, soapmakers, millers, carpenters, machinists, masons and printers found places alongside the farmers.[10] The majority of young men probably didn't go very far to work, however. Most labored on their parents' farm or worked for someone else in a nearby shop.

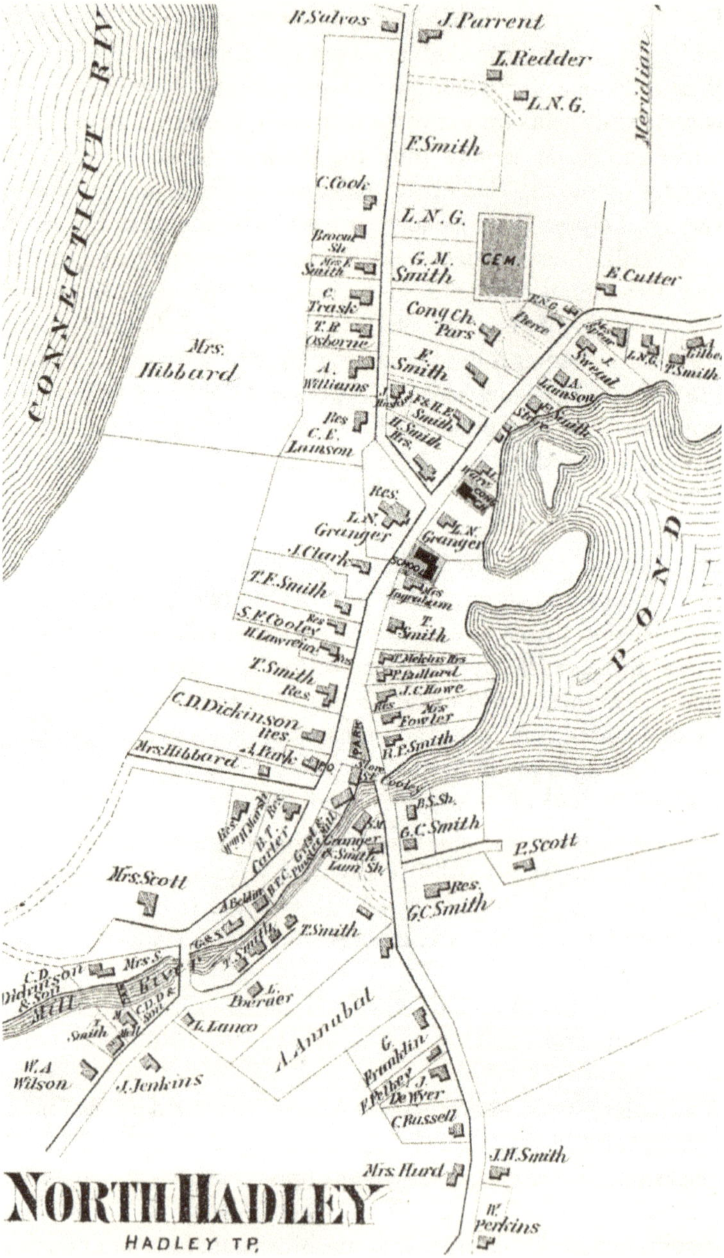

Figure 2: North Hadley in 1860.
County Atlas of Hampshire, Massachusetts. From Actual Surveys by and under the Direction o F.W. Beers (New York: F.W. Beers, 1860).

Many also went to school. A few boys even studied law in hopes of becoming lawyers. Hadley had several new immigrants before the war and a few blacks. It's encouraging to look at their locations in town and realize that they were in no way segregated. Even when newcomers lived together, such grouping was not forced upon them. French Street in North Hadley once housed many of the Canadian broom makers who, apparently, chose that location for their homes. It appeared as though Hadley was to be the setting for a Norman Rockwell painting.[11]

Although there do not seem to be local accounts of daily life, *The Diary of a Binghamton Boy* tells the routine of Morris Treadwell, a boy living on a farm on the outskirts of a small city in upstate

A STREET IN HADLEY.

Figure 3: Mr. Kilburn, "A Street in Hadley"
Ballou's Pictorial Drawing-Room Companion 8.12 (24 March 1855) 184.

The model of a town worth defending. Hadley here displayed its commitment to civil law (Town Hall) and communal piety (First Congregational Church). Out of sight to the picture's right stood the third pillar of an admirable New England town, Hopkins Academy. The carefully tended trees hinted at the agricultural richness. The road sign and purposeful ox cart connoted successful commerce. The dapper carriage heading south on the historic mile-long common suggested the possibility of prosperity for everyone.

New York during the 1860s.[12] He recalls splitting kindling and going to church services, killing mice and attending a county fair, drawing manure out of barn yards and enjoying sleigh rides and square dances. His world was small, perhaps, but full. He speaks of injuring himself and recovering. He does not lose his head when people die. He enjoys numbers: how many dollars hay costs, how much his father sells butter for, how many pounds he weighs. His responsibilities and pleasures no doubt mirror those of a boy in Hadley. Neither Morris nor his peers in my town could imagine what history held in store for them.

Chapter Two
Many Calls to Arms

On 12 April 1861, the island of Fort Sumter absorbed heavy fire from the angry rebel batteries on the mainland of Charleston, South Carolina. After thirty-four hours, the Union commander, Major Robert Anderson, surrendered to his former pupil at West Point, Pierre Beauregard. The Union soldiers marched away unharmed; the only casualty had been one confederate horse.[13] President Lincoln pleaded with the northern population to enlist and less than four months later the first Hadley volunteer, George H. Williams, complied.[14] In the following years, 232 other boys from Hadley would enlist.[15] Three families of blacks in town sent over half their men to fight for freedom.[16] Although they all travelled many miles from the secure Pioneer Valley, they kept in touch with their families and neighbors. Heroic and touching stories about residents' sons fighting far away reached Hadley via letters and reports that were published regularly (and apparently uncensored) in *The Hampshire Gazette and Northampton Courier*, a four-page weekly newspaper printed in nearby Northampton.

The reasons that moved boys to enlist sound simple but, to early twentieth-first-century realists, rather surprising. Like most towns, Hadley didn't want war; however, they strongly

ATTENTION !

VOLUNTEERS !

E N L I S T

AND

AVOID THE DRAFT.

$452 BOUNTY !

AND STATE AID !

Every Volunteer has his Choice
of Regiments.

THE following Generous Bounties are now offered to Veteran Soldiers who have served Nine months in the Union Armies and been honorably discharged, and who shall enlist for three years or the war, payable in installments as follows:—

State Bounty,	- -	$50
First Installment,	-	60
Premium,	- - -	2
One Month's Pay,	-	13
Advance Payment, -	-	125

Figure 4: Advertisement for volunteers in the *Hampshire Gazette and Northampton Courier* 24 November 1863, page 3, column 7.

On top of flagstaff is the Roman *pileus*, or freedom cap, symbol of an emancipated slave.

favored restoration of the Union and, once secession became a fact, were willing to fight to crush rebellion. Many northerners initially considered slavery a side issue.[17] In those early days of the struggle against disunion, the public reacted in the same way. At a town meeting on Friday, 3 May 1861, people agreed that while they "lament the necessity of the present war against the sister States of our republic We are fixed in the determination by all the money and means in our power to support it until we obtain an honarable [sic] peace."[18] Throughout the memoir of Hadley resident H. Clement Russell shines this burning desire to re-unite the nation in which he had grown to young manhood. When he recalls seeing "a large number of" former slaves "laughing, singing, weeping, dancing" around President Lincoln, he doesn't comment on how proud he feels to have freed them. Instead he says, "[W]e had accomplished a great work.... [W]e had been trying for four years to get Richmond, the capital of the Southern Confederacy."[19] Russell implies that reuniting the union and destroying the rebels was far more important to him than freeing the slaves.

Russell's feelings about why he fought seem to reflect the feelings of a majority of volunteers. In *Billy Yank*, a 1978 book about the life of a typical Union soldier, northerners repeatedly express their "antipathy toward

Negroes."[20] One soldier used the derogatory vernacular of the 1860s to say with disgust, "I don't think enough of the Niggar to go and fight for them. I would rather fight them." Many people today believe the Civil War was fought primarily to free the black slaves. It is an appealing idea, one half of America fighting its evil twin in order to bring equality to all races. But many believed that the North's main ambition was, in words that became familiar from their repetition in the newspaper, to "see the maintenance of the Union."[21] While northerners were not sympathetic toward slavery, they still had their reservations about African Americans. A Union soldier wrote from Beaufort, North Carolina, for the enlightenment of readers living near Northampton, "Some of these fellows work very well, but generally they are on the watch to escape the eye of the overseer and be off out of the way of all work." The writer felt that former slaves were not good prospects for citizenship because he believed they "are ignorant and indolent."[22]

Most people in Hadley agreed with their liberal counterparts in centers of abolition like Boston that slavery was wrong, but they hated secession more and desired to reunite the Union. Thus, during the first two years or so of the crusade, the town had little trouble meeting their quota of required draftees. This patriotism may seem odd. After all, there are a variety of reasons to explain why people in an out-of-the-way town would prefer not to get involved. First, most families farmed and needed men around the house. The idea of losing even one hand might have cooled most ideas of travelling to some distant state no matter how noble the reason. Also people preferred to come to the Connecticut Valley rather than leave it. The weather, compared to that of more northern or southern states, was often pleasant, the fields fertile, jobs could be had and the economy was diverse. In addition, enlistees at first received no bounty and later, around 1863, only a small one. Whereas volunteers in Binghamton, New York, could sometimes earn $1,500 for their bounties, Hadley never gave more than $150.[23]

Despite these reasons to stay home, men of all ages flocked to volunteer. Various religious services reminded citizens about the war and played on their hearts to make them enlist. "War sermons" were popular. "Our brave ones died gloriously and not in vain," preached the Reverend Mr. Clark for Thanksgiving 1862. "The time has come," he said, "when pointed sentences must give way to pointed steel."[24] His ferocity echoes that of other clergymen who often spoke for nearly an hour but kept their audiences' attention when they urged a holy war for "the subjugation of traitors."[25] Several sermons criticized slavery, a practice that one was expected to reject: when the noted professor of Classics at Amherst College William Seymour Tyler spoke at the Russell Church in Hadley, he delivered "a strong anti-slavery sermon, delivered to just as strong an anti-slavery people."[26]

At the same time that ministers reminded audiences of their religious duties, political leaders stirred up patriotism by using language that sounded equally religious. Senator Charles Sumner spoke in Worcester, and the *Hampshire Gazette* covered his speech. He blasted the rebels, comparing their mutiny to Satan's "upon the Almighty."[27] The connection between church and town hall surfaces when Hadley people voted on 19 July 1862 to present $100 to each volunteer and then resolved "that the most devoted, godly christian will be the most truly patriotic and dutiful citizen."[28]

At the same time that pastors and politicians talked about ideals, the newspaper featured reports about local men who had fallen to rebel shells, further touching Hadley citizens. As the war ground on, lists of casualties frequently appeared. Usually only a name and place indicated that some boy would never return: "Great Battle at Newbern, N. C.... James Sullivan, Hadley, mortally."[29] Other times, the notice contained more details, adding to the pain: "Death of Myron Newton, 26, of Hadley ... shot through the breast. He never spoke after receiving the fatal ball."[30] Many of the deaths came indirectly from disease. The sad obituary of the *Hampshire Gazette* for 5 May 1863: 2, 5 reads,

Died – In Hospital at Baton Rouge, La. April 20 of typhoid fever, Charles W. Clark, son of Theodore Clark of Hadley, aged 23. He went with the regiment on the march to Port Hudson, and immediately on returning was sent to the hospital. He was not considered seriously ill until a short time of his death.

Figure 5: Thomas Nast, "Southern Chivalry"
Harper's Weekly 7.319 (7 February 1863) 88-89.

The attack on Fort Sumpter in Charleston Harbor began a tradition of mistrusting Rebel morality. So many accusations of Confederate atrocities barraged Northern ears that the entire region lost its claim to civilization. Relentless propaganda accused southerners of committing unspeakable horrors.

Unexpected deaths from bullets or disease, moving as they were, did not inflame readers as much as tales of "secesh" treachery. The newspaper routinely reported how outrageously the enemy acted. One "reb" pretended to surrender to George C. Marshall, a former Hadley resident, then shot him and fled. Marshall lingered two painful days before dying.[31] "[A] rebel fiend," begged by a wounded Union man for help, placed "his rifle at his throat ... , saying 'I will cure you, you son of a bitch'" and murdered the fallen soldier.[32]

Figure 6: Thomas Nast, "After the Battle – the Rebels in Possession of the Field" *Harper's Weekly* 6.304 (25 October 1862) 680-81.

Propaganda also asserted that "Secesh" troops obeyed no civilized laws. Here they despoil fallen soldiers after a raid in Maryland. Other accusations against Southern barbarism included bayoneting wounded Union troops after a skirmish (*Harper's Weekly* 5.242 [17 August 1861] 525), using savage dogs to pursue unarmed Unionists, lynching anti-slavery partisans, displacing women, children, the crippled and the elderly from their homes, using Indians to scalp Abolitionists, murdering a father and daughter in their living room (the previous five examples in *Frank Leslie's Illustrated Newspaper* 16.393 [4 April 1863] 25).

Even after death, the newspaper said, northern troops could expect "acts of sacrilege as to excite the indignation of Christian men everywhere" from the unchivalrous southerners.[33] Also, who would not want to do something after reading an atrocity article that claimed that "the head of one of our most gallant officers was cut off by a secessionist, to be used as a drinking cup"?[34] The newspaper promoted an image of the southerners' inhumanity by comparing these acts of white men to crimes "never committed by savage islanders, or a tribe of Choctaws or Blackfeet."[35]

AN UNWELCOME RETURN.

THREE MONTHS' VOLUNTEER. "What! don't you know me—your own husband?"
DAUGHTER OF COLUMBIA. "Get away! No husband of mine would be here while the country needs his help."

Figure 7: *Harper's Weekly* 5.241 (10 August 1861) 510.

Humor complemented atrocity images in the campaign to attract volunteers. The stock figures of a feisty younger wife and an older husband of dubious courage conveyed the patriotic message, and was meant to pressure prospective volunteers.

Visual persuasions to march to war surrounded Hadleyites as mainstream publications like *Harper's Weekly* printed drawings of atrocities like emaciated prisoners, and even a necklace made from a Union soldier's teeth. We can reconstruct the imaginative world that influenced these innocents by viewing the same illustrations they saw in popular magazines such as *Frank Leslie's Illustrated Newspaper* and *Ballou's*. Like *Collier's, Life* and *The Saturday Evening Post* in the next century, these mass circulation weeklies brought a large world into uncounted households. Anti-secessionist propaganda insisted on the barbarity of slave owners. It also condemned Confederates who looted the Union dead after battles or starved helpless prisoners. Sinister accusations that the South employed Indians to commit atrocities must have especially moved lads who had grown up hearing the legend of the Angel of Hadley and seeing the current North Hadley mill, whose 1677 predecessor had been burned by Native Americans.

The longer the conflict lasted, the more the "Johnies" or "sesech men" were portrayed as less than human. Memories of terrible prisons like the Libey at Richmond, Virginia, and Andersonville, Georgia, depressed and angered those who had survived. Even if the northern victims were unknown, the accounts aimed to spur any reader to want revenge. One man described the "inhuman and heathenish treatment toward our gallant boys" confined to Libey Prison by brutish jailors. (Hadley man Augustus Dickinson suffered in Libey.[36]) Another survivor talked touchingly of the foul misery at Andersonville, where Hadley sons Elisha Bigelow, George Boice, Charles Howard and Warren Russell perished. Especially in Hadley, which continued to build comfortable homes during the conflict, such exposés inflamed people.[37]

The pain lasted far after the fighting. In 1910 H. Clement Russell, who recalled most of his war-time experiences without anger, composed an essay concerning "The Captain From Belle Island," the confederate prison camp in Richmond, Virginia. There Union prisoners went without food from Saturday night to Monday morning. In his memoir, Russell describes how he went to the Philadelphia Centennial Exposition in 1877 and recognized his former jailor, the "great big blackbearded captain with a big roaring voice." Russell

Figure 8: "The Boston Regiments Embarking for Washington in the Jersey City Cars" *Harper's Weekly* 5.227 (4 May 1861) 280.

went up to him and said, "I used to eat to your boarding house on Belle Isle." When the commandant tried to excuse his behavior ("But, suh, we didn't have anything to eat ourselves"), Russell sneered, "the more shame to you that you didn't quit sooner'n you did."[38]

The terrible reports published during the war gave some men reason enough to enlist. (As the man who described Libey said, "If this war was to last a thousand years, I pray God to spare me life and limb to fight rebels. I wish to do nothing until the last one is exterminated.") Yet even without the religion, politics and atrocity propaganda, social pressures urged Hadley men to take destiny into their own hands, sign the enlistment form and train to fill the rebels' "bellies full" with hot lead.[39] Newspapers told of mass gatherings where older men like Hadley resident "Horace Vanhorn, with his gray head and fifty years firmly stepped upon the stand and put down his name."[40] Like revival meetings, these "large and enthusiastic" assemblies swept people up in their emotion.[41] Once mustered into the service, the new recruits received extra notice. Where else would simple farm boys cause "immense" crowds to assemble and cheer "enthusiastically" as they marched along?[42] Teenagers and young adults who ordinarily never hoped to do anything different from their fathers were told that recruits elected many of their own officers.[43] What an unexpected chance to make something of one's self! As if this sudden star status was not enough reason to enlist, the boys had some economic motive. Especially after President Lincoln called for 300,000 additional troops in 1862 and 500,000 more in 1864, communities and states offered bounties to sign up.[44] Although the salaries of volunteers varied from county to county, they seem small to us today.[45] Still, how many boys in their late teens had ready cash?

Bell Irvin Wiley's classic study *Billy Yank* says that the main reason the war seemed so attractive was the lure of far away places.[46] Most early travel accounts sent home by local men sound like ads for a vacation on a cruise ship. As the 10th sailed to Washington, troopers saw "occasionally a school of porpoises, and sometimes the boys would imagine they could see a whale spouting in the distance."[47] Even when exotic creatures were hidden, men of the 27th obviously enjoyed their chance to cruise along "the beautiful scenery which characterizes the banks of the Hudson ... [and] the Delaware river just at sunrise."⁴⁸ And if scenery was not enough, northern correspondents populated the south with appealing natives. A writer with the 10th in Washington said, "There are any quantity of negroes here, old and young, big and little. Every morning the women come round with milk, eggs all boiled, fried fish, hoe cakes, meat, pies, cakes, blackberries, ice cream, lemonade, and almost anything you want to eat; they sell everything cheap, too." Adding to the picnic atmosphere, he continues, "as I sit in my tent a perfect re-production of Topsy [the merry slave girl in Harriet Beecher Stowe's novel *Uncle Tom's Cabin*] is amusing the soldiers by her antics."⁴⁹ For boys who entertained themselves at home by digging out foxes⁵⁰ and woodchucks⁵¹, or who had seen blacks only as co-workers, such accounts must have been magnetic.

Imaginative pictures of what war was like also bombarded the wavering civilian. In one story published in the *Hampshire Gazette*, a Seneca Indian loyal to the Union imitated the main characters of James Fenimore Cooper's novels by camouflaging himself with pine boughs, creeping under a tree in which a rebel sharpshooter lurked and, when the enemy had to reload, ordering him to surrender.⁵² In another stirring description, an author identified only as W. H. C. made the battle in April 1863 at White Oak Church, Virginia, sound like some heroic fantasy:

> The word is given, the men spring up from behind the railroad and the line advances double quick. Grape pours in our ranks a raking fire, – from behind rifle pits leaps blaze after blaze, – through our devoted line comes crashing on the shot and shell, – many a gap is rent, but still on they go, – the fire comes thicker and faster, – the men are scattered, – they waver! What a moment of awful suspense! ... One regiments breaks in confusion, – the[y] fly! God forbid, – they are coming back. But no, the foremost line is true, – the shattered ranks press nobly on – the flying regiment rallies, – our boys have gained the rifle pits, – bayonets flash and plunge, – our colors are planted now, – deafening cheers arise – we send them back – the walls ring – the rebels fly – but see them fall beneath their pursuers!"⁵³

The fact that Hadley's Henry Fales died at White Oak Church or that his neighbors Warren Lyman and Samuel Thayer suffered such severe injuries that they were discharged on the spot does not restrain W. H. C. With similar jauntiness, a third press agent (named "Cyrus") transformed the exhaustion and fear of military life into some boy scout anecdote: a soldier near Newbern, North Carolina, fell asleep during a break in the march. The 27th accidentally left him behind. He awoke surrounded by rebels, lay low, watched as an African American found his rifle and turned it in to the southerners. After three days "wandering through the Swups," he rejoined his regiment, no more the worse for wear, apparently, and full of a good story to tell.[54]

Lurking in the background of these glorified pictures was the hint of things to steal. Soldiers took food and firewood on marches, an act probably unthinkable at home, but made glamorous when one is in Louisiana: "Men march along with loads of poultry meat and sugar for the evening meal. When we bivouac at night, the fences come down… and the camp fires stretching along for miles with songs and revelry present a pleasant and animated scene… [which] is very romantic and all seem to enjoy it."[55] In addition to liberated food, souvenirs soon became common. A writer with the 10th noted that even after defeat at Bull Run, the escapees "all have some trophy, taken on the battle field."[56] Men of the 27th sent home a number of keepsakes including Confederate flags, muskets, Bowie knives and "an elegant corkscrew."[57] One can still see the trophies saved by H. Clement Russell, now displayed in the Historical Room of Goodwin Memorial Library: the musket used by his friend William R. Montague to capture six rebel soldiers, Confederate money, Russell's tent and coffee bag and "a piece of bacon, pretty well dried out after all these years."[58]

Perhaps more attractive than portable objects, the prospect of possessing land once farmed by secessionists beckoned recruits. Though Hadley was reasonably prosperous, only ten men earned incomes of over $10,000.[59] Therefore a description of "The Abandoned Plantations on the Mississippi River" that appeared in the *Hampshire Gazette* must have lured at least some attention when it promised, "A man who takes on eighty acres can go back home at the end of the year with at least eight thousand dollars in his pocket. Would he make one-tenth that by staying at home?"[60]

Chapter Three

Who Answered the Calls?

The combined inducements of church, government, atrocity propaganda, romance and money worked, but only for a while. The figures show that the longer the war lasted, the fewer home boys signed up. In the first year of war, 1861, 20 out of the 222 eligible Hadley men enlisted their services. What is more surprising, 39 volunteers who were not on the eligibility list joined in 1861. Of these 59 men who volunteered, only six were over 26 years old, while 33% (19 men) were between 23 and 26 years old. The conglomeration of 20-22 year olds, probably the biggest help on the farm because they were relatively mature and most likely still single, almost matches the number of 23-26 year olds. Eighteen 20-22 year olds enlisted, about 31% of the men who enlisted that year. The remaining 18% (11 men) left home to restore the Union before their twentieth birthday. Families like the Williams sent four young men, while others like the Billings sent just one.[61]

Although 59 enlistments do not sound overwhelmingly patriotic, consider Hadley's size and primary occupation. With just 2,230 men, women and children, every hand counted. If a young man chose to leave his household, he usually joined a company of the 27th or 37th Massachusetts Volunteer Infantry. These regiments, along with the 10th and 20th, absorbed the majority of local recruits. In Massachusetts, African American men served in the famous 54th regiment, the Robert Gould Shaw unit featured in the movie *Glory*. In these units, men agreed to serve for a three-year tour. And since October 1862, potential soldiers had a chance to enlist in the 52nd for a nine-month obligation. In July 1863, when national conscription was instituted, one could wait to be drafted, could pay a commutation fee if drafted or could furnish a substitute.

In 1862, a slightly larger number of eligible men enlisted. Maybe the small increase resulted from those who wanted to revenge a friend or help finish an increasingly ugly war. This year, 36 out of the 243 eligible males enlisted. Unlike 1861, when more ineligible candidates enlisted, only 29 males who were not on the eligibility list volunteered. The ages of the soldiers, however, differed greatly. Whereas in '61, the larger portion of the troops was in their middle twenties, 23-26, in 1862, younger men signed their names. Overall, 52% of the volunteers from Hadley that year were under 22 years old. And in 1861 only 6% of the men were over 26 (Theodore Billings and Willard Hibbard were over 40), but in 1862 about 27% of the men were over 27.

1862 was also an odd draft year. The war needed tough, mature yet still young men to beat the "tall, thin, sickly looking" rebels.[62] But the enlistees were not the capable adults that the army required. Instead, they were the young who wanted adventure. If they weren't kids, then they were aging adults who might better have rallied on the troops as they passed through town rather than fighting with them. H. Clement Russell recalled the older man who rejuvenated the spirits of troopers in F/37 with a rousing pep talk as they marched near Gettysburg: "Boys, those d – – d rebels have stolen all my cows, my horses and my hens, and when you get there I hope you give 'em hell!"[63]

The following year, 1863, more puzzling enlistees appeared on the rolls. While only 14 men joined, some 36% of the men were under 20. There was no one over 30, and only three between 23 and 26 signed up.[64]

The year 1864 continued the pattern of the young and old joining. 38% percent of the enlistees were under 22 and another 38% were older than 27. Only 37 men from Hadley went south to fight. True, there was an increase of 23 men from 1863, but a decrease of about 30 men from 1862. Maybe Hadley realized that their boys might come back in less than perfect health or not at all.

The final year of the war, 1865, reflected Hadley's fading interest in the bloody conflict. With 229 men eligible to fight in the war, not a single man on the list signed up. A paltry four men enlisted, three of whom were between 20 and 22 years old. Out of these four, one man never joined his unit, so only three men from Hadley fought alongside the remaining Union soldiers.

The number of deserters increased, too, reflecting the odd way of recording a recruit's town. One might have been born in Hadley, have been living here but born elsewhere, or been born and residing in some other town yet credited to Hadley's quota. Truman Meekins was home grown: he appears in records before, during and after the war. (He must have been quite a character. Before he joined H/52 in October 1862, Meekins fired the big village cannon from the doorway of his barn and, as the *Hampshire Gazette* for 25 February 1862 says, "set fire to a quantity of loose hay on the barn floor.")

Men like Narzar Benoit and Leander Belleville obviously came down from Canada to fashion brooms yet suffered for their adopted country. A third class of men like Concklin, Cowan, Meyer and Warren felt no loyalty to Hadley or to their original home towns and, for one reason or another, deserted. Boundaries which look so clear on maps of the period apparently meant little. Even after the conflict had ended, officials walked ("perambulated") the border between Hadley and Sunderland in 1865[65] and tried to coordinate efforts with officials in South Hadley so the two towns would have a marker on Mount Holyoke showing where the line was.[66]

Men here and in nearby towns increasingly paid commutation money or sent substitutes. North Amherst men who were eligible formed a club to guard against the draft. Each of the 80 members subscribed $7.50 so that, when any was drafted, each could receive the $300 commutation fee.[67] Another common practice involved going to a large city and finding enough men there to enlist under the local quota. The newspaper tells how four blacks had been found in Washington who were willing to join instead of four Amherst men.[68] The practice of avoiding service became so common that celebrities bragged about it. The famous public speaker "Edward Everett ... sent two recruits to represent him in the army." The article added, with no irony, "He believes in securing peace by fighting for it."[69] The Civil War faded from passionate oratory to sad resignation to obvious avoidance. During the drought of 1864, the "dusty road, withered grass" and possible crop failure occupied people's attention.[70] Through fall and January 1865, papers focused on efforts to repeal a tax on leaf tobacco and barely mentioned the distant hostilities.[71]

Chapter Four

Why Did Enthusiasm Die?

The decreasing number of local enlistees and increasing percentage of men recruited from outside the town trigger the question: why was Hadley hesitant to sacrifice more men to what had started as a universally applauded campaign? Like any crusade, even this one which sounded so noble when described by ministers, politicians and recent inductees, reality eventually depressed people's eagerness to participate directly.

First, the facts about army life reached home. Several volunteers neutrally recorded typical days: "reveile is sounded in our camp every morning at 6 1/2 o'clock, roll call 6 3/4, breakfast at 7, guard mounting at 9, company drill at 9 1/2, dinner at 12 pm."[72]

Such regularity might not have disturbed some farm boys, but the unexpected took its toll. The transportation that once sounded like Caribbean cruises sometimes turned into nightmares. A local boy on his way to join Burnside's expedition in Hatteras Inlet, North Carolina, wrote: "Every man of the regiment ... was sea sick.... The men suffered much.... They all expected to go to the bottom ... we can have no adequate conceptions of the sufferings and danger which our poor fellows were obliged to go through."[73]

Once Hadley men arrived at their destination, the wretched weather often appalled them. Letter after letter mentions rain and mud that made sleeping miserable and travel agony. Reports of foul weather made the south seem like some alien planet. A typical note from a local boy groans, "It was raining all the time, as it had been all day.... Every thing wet through, feet almost raw ... Oh! such mud!"[74] Once the rain stopped, the hot southern sun took its toll. Letters repeat the same complaint (this expressed by a trooper from the 27th near Richmond, Virginia): "The heat was intense on Saturday, and we suffered more from the sun than the bullets. Not less than one hundred and sixty were prostrated in our brigade by sunstroke."[75] For Hadley boys who grew up near the Connecticut River and Lake Warner, arid new landscapes were especially hostile: "Frequently men [from the 37th, marching through New Baltimore, Virginia] have to go a mile or more for water."[76]

And even if the weather had been perfect, the heavy uniform – the same uniform that people applauded during marches to the nearby railroad station – would have been burdensome. A typical load for a man in the 37th included a "knapsack, heavily laden. Everyone had an overcoat, woolen blanket, rubber blanket, a dress coat or blouse, 2 or 3 pairs of stockings, as many extra shirts, a pair of drawers, shoes, with brush and blacking, a good supply of writing material ... and the whole made a load of some 70 or 75 pounds – an unmerciful load for the soldier."[77] The average age of soldiers was 25; the typical man stood 5'8" tall and weighed 143 pounds.[78] So this pack weighed half as much as the trooper carrying it.

Weather and weight helped to exhaust otherwise fit farm boys. So did the unpredictable maneuvers. Captain Parsons of C/10 described how his group lived near Chickahominy, Virginia: "we formed lines at six in the morning, and it was past midnight when we stacked arms and unslung knapsacks, to rest. The boys were all tired out."[79] Likewise the food available contradicted those picnic lunches described in early letters. Accounts of hunger and thirst became frequent and distressing. One man from the 10th found near Winesburg, Virginia, a rebel knapsack with crackers and bits of ham: "I confiscated it; oh, how good it tasted. I did not stop to think whether it belonged to a dead or live man it was all the same to me."[80]

News of battles where thousands died reached Hadley. Even if one did not know any of the fallen, the papers suggested that something had changed in the war. When first declared, the war inspired many patriotic poems with titles like "The American Hero,"[81] "Hymn to Liberty" and "Thy Will Be Done."[82] The first one dismissed the tragedy of death: "Life for my country and the cause of Freedom, / Is but a trifle for a worm to part with." Other early verse claimed that "New England's Dead" had "rushed to battle" during the Revolution and been granted victory.[83] As uncensored accounts of so many casualties returned, however, the poems became more somber. They tried to make sense of the incredible slaughter, yet the titles still reminded readers of death. "The Dying Soldier" lies all night after being wounded in combat, waiting for the morning when angels will come for his soul.[84] Mrs. R. B. Edson's "The Unreturning Brave" concentrates on the farm and woods that "shall know him nevermore!"[85] Even when "Our Heroes," in a poem by Francis De Haes Janvier, are assured that a "chaplet unfading / Shall bind every brow," there is small comfort to those who survive.[86]

These increasingly somber fictional works paralleled factual accounts of deaths. Certainly reports of men uttering patriotic last words as they died continued. Early and late, home folks were treated to noble sentiments like, "I die for my country" (this is from a trooper in C/10 during 1862)[87] and "I fear I shall not live, but I tried to do my duty, and if I die it is in my country's cause" (H/27, 1865).[88] However, the same notices that conveyed such inspiring self-sacrifice must have frightened those who considered joining the army. After the battle of White Oak Church, Virginia, a writer claimed that a man from the 37th was happy he received "nothing but a flesh wound" because "then I shall have another chance at them; they'll pay dearly for this."[89] The description of the surroundings makes the boy's heroism less appealing:

> [T]he day is ours. Look at that bloody field! See those mangled forms. It is a fearful price to pay. The wounded men came pouring in. The street was crowded with ambulances. The air was filled with groans, some begging for a drop of water, some praying to die that they might be out of agony. Blood in the streets – blood on the sidewalks – blood in the halls – blood everywhere.[90]

Many soldiers saw enough suffering to want escape. Yet as Dr. Greene of the 52nd explained, medical discharges were next to impossible to obtain: "While there is anything left of a soldier they will keep him."[91] The one way to avoid such horror was to refuse enlistment.

Perhaps the information that hurt the most and made more people hesitant about enlisting told of local men who had been killed or wounded or sent to the hospital because of illness. Disaster is always more painful when you know the person involved. Sometimes readers at home learned how untruthful optimistic reports could be. When Levi Dickinson was sent to the hospital near Fredericksburg, Virginia, the paper said he was "considered on the improve"; on 17 January 1864, obviously broken by his ordeal, Dickinson was permanently discharged because of his disability.[92] Other dispatches of a local boy's last moments drove home how absurd killing can be. The widow Scott, one of North Hadley's wealthiest citizens, might not have taken much comfort from this obituary in the *Hampshire Gazette*:

> Orderly Sergeant Aaron Scott, son of the late Rufus Scott of North Hadley, serving as a volunteer in the 96th Ill. regt., near Atlanta, Ga., was killed by a random shot from the enemy while reclining in a tent, reading his testament on the 2nd inst. The *Waukegan Gazette* says, "We have been shown several letters from the field before Atlanta, all uniting in testifying that Sergeant Scott as a soldier was brave to a fault, as a patriot true as steel, and as a Christian's bright and shining light." His death casts a gloom over his native village.[93]

Scott's decency did not preserve him. As if to underline the randomness of luck, the column containing this account also tells how the citizens of Columbus, Mississippi, presented "a valuable sword" to Aaron's town mate Isaiah H. Williams, then Provost Marshall of the captured city.

People preferred to talk about the weather in the Connecticut Valley for the good reason that war news from distant battlefields depressed Hadley. Out of the 179 men who enlisted in Hadley and the 54 men like T.S. Billings who joined up with Amherst or other surrounding towns,[94] 15% died. Some 35 (counting the other town enlistees) young, healthy, needed boys fell to the hardships of war. It was far more common for a lad to die of disease then it was by bullet. "In the federal forces," one account says, "four persons died of sickness for everyone killed in battle, and deaths from disease were twice those resulting from all other known causes."[95] People at home knew the double dangers. Levi Stockbridge wrote his son Francis, who had survived the slaughter of other men in F/37 at the Bloody Angle, Spottsylvania, Virginia, on 22 May 1864, saying, "Thank God you are yet safe and pray that in all perils his watchful care may yet be over you, shielding you from sickness and the traitor's aim."[96] All told, 40%, or 93 men, came back to Hadley wounded, dead or former prisoners of war. These numbers are staggering. Think about how small Hadley was. The awful adventure destroyed or injured 93 valuable men because they agreed, for various reasons, to serve their country.

Chapter Five

Real People

In war, the names of most soldiers remain mere names. Only relatives recall George Boice, Rufus Cook and Daniel Howard, three men from Hadley who sacrificed their lives. No one thinks that they might have single-handedly turned the tide of the war. They most likely could not have. They must have died like most other men: tired, hungry, in pain and scared. Yet each one of the 35 men who died had a history. They had families and memories just like Grant and Lincoln did. But still, they never achieved fame.

A. Joseph Hooker

One man from Hadley became well-known. Joseph Hooker, better known to his men as "fighting Joe," was born on 13 November 1814 in Hadley, on West Street.[97] He graduated from Hopkins Academy, less than 1/2 mile away. Although his family encouraged him, he really never wanted to be a military person. Instead, Hooker dreamed of becoming a lawyer. But in 1833, after passing the entrance exam to West Point, the 18-year-old Hadley native left his serene town to begin his career as a soldier. Things didn't shape up in Hooker's favor when he arrived at the academy, however. He was a smart student who "ranked well above the average in final grades," but he had so many demerits, given to students for "violations of post rules, lack of proper respect for superiors, inattentiveness in class etc, ... that his final rank after four years was 29th out of 50 cadets."[98] This class standing determined what grade officer one would be. Hooker first became a commissioned second lieutenant in the 1st Artillery, then bounced around, even returning to West Point as an adjutant until he finally made his way up to General. According to gossip, he loved alcohol and women. Because he always made sure that his men had plenty of food, blankets and clothes, as well as strong drink and females, the troops adored him. If politicians had sounded like preachers when they talked of the war, Hooker's admirers made him seem to be a saint: "Our badge was Hooker's star. The corps was swallowed up in its General.... [H]is presence was worth a dozen regiments. It gave courage to the timid, strength to the weary, hope to the despondent, almost life to the dead."[99]

Unfortunately, he was unlucky in the field. During the battle of Chancellorsville, in May 1863, Hooker had twice as many men as the rebels led by Robert E. Lee. For some reason Hooker failed to engage the Confederates. A cannon ball shattered a pillar on the porch of Hooker's command house and apparently dazed him. At least that excuse saves him from worse charges. Just as Hooker's men, President Lincoln liked Joe. Instead of punishing him for his faulty judgment in battle, Lincoln simply re-assigned him to lesser positions. The respect seemed mutual: Hooker led the funeral procession when Lincoln was assassinated.

No matter how poorly Hooker performed during battle, people in Hadley loved him. When he returned for holidays, the townspeople referred to him as the "beautiful cadet."[100] Hooker's good looks seemed to sweep everyone off their feet. An observer in Rhode Island said he was "one of the handsomest men the army ever produced."[101] Hooker never resettled in Hadley; he lived the rest of his years in California, New Hampshire, New York and Washington. On 31 October 1879, he died suddenly in Garden City, Long Island, and was buried in Spring Grove Cemetery, Cincinnati, Ohio. Reportedly the audience at his funeral was surpassed only by the audiences at the funerals of Abraham Lincoln and Horace Greeley.[102]

Figure 9: "Major-General Hooker, Commanding the Army of the Potomac"
Harper's Weekly 7.322 (28 February 1863) 129 [front cover].

Hooker's likeness appeared frequently in large-circulation magazines as well as
on sheet music and in newspapers.

Figure 10: Edwin Forbes, "Battle of Chancellorsville, Sunday, May 8—General Hooker Repulsing the Attack of the Enemy"
Frank Leslie's Illustrated Newspaper 16.399 (23 May 1863) 137.

Panoramic illustrations of battles were the staple of popular publications. The introduction of the balloon expanded artists' spatial imaginations. (See "Balloon View of the Attack on Fort Darling in the James River." *Harper's Weekly* 6.283 [31 May 1862] 337 [cover].) Yet the majority of pictures adhered to classical ideas of balanced composition and heroic posture. These proportioned engravings could not possibly recreate the chaos, blinding smoke, deafening noise and pain of conflict, but they painted a picture of heroism also meant to attract volunteers.

B. H. Clement Russell

While realistic reports from the newspaper flooded into Hadley, telling about famous men and major battles, one local man stored up memories. In 1918, H. Clement Russell set down a 40-page account of happenings some 53 years after the conclusion of the war. Even though Russell was now 62 years old, his chronicle of the war seems accurate when compared to the 25,000 diaries used by Bell Irvin Wiley to write *The Life Of Billy Yank*. Russell's record matches the brief synopsis about a few men's feelings that prefaces *The History of the Thirty-Seventh*. Russell's war stories do not have a "big fish" ring to them. Instead they report the war modestly and honestly. The entries don't venture deep into

Russell's subconscious, yet they relate the war in a more detailed fashion than the newspapers. There are some sections, like when Russell tells about receiving orders to shoot as fast as possible at the rebels (24), that might have been included in *Billy Yank* when it says that the Union guns would become "so hot from the rapid firing as to make them temporarily unusable."[103] When Russell talks about the grueling marches, which sometimes amounted to 44 miles in one day, and the rigors of military life, *Billy Yank* and the *Hampshire Gazette* mirror these claims with similar hardships of army life. *Billy Yank* talks about having to report to roll call as many as 26 times a day, for example. Russell tells about the different battles he fought in like Gettysburg and Cold Harbor. After suffering wounds to the head in the battle of the Wilderness in 1864, he spent nine months recuperating. During his stay in the hospital, Russell reports the same grim, unsanitary conditions that *Billy Yank* describes: "Hogs belonging to the Farm eating arms and other portions of the body"[104] outside the medical tent; Russell himself was almost buried when, weak from loss of blood, he collapsed outside the amputating tent, near "more than a wheel-barrow load of arms, hands and legs."[105]

Clement Russell not only speaks for the typical soldier, he also symbolizes the loyal Hadley man. On his way back to the hospital, Russell encountered a group of soldiers known as "stragglers," "bummers" and "coffee coolers." These cowardly men sat in the rear of the army and never attempted to move to the front line. Coming from a town like Hadley, where neighbors pitched in to complete a project, he couldn't understand why men who had enlisted and marched and engaged the enemy, just like he had, now refused to fight. Russell naturally felt "disgusted" after seeing the "Army in the rear who would not 'face the music.'" In Hadley, he knew, townspeople supported each other: when Edmund Burke's three year old son played with matches and accidentally burned down "barns filled with tobacco and hay," the *Hampshire Gazette* assumed "that the liberality of the Hadley people will be manifested in replacing, in part, at least his losses."[106] This idea of togetherness helped Russell to triumph over hardship.

C. John Dunbar and *Dances With Wolves*

While Joseph P. Hooker's life story was written by Walter H. Herbert and Clement Russell was immortalized by his own diaries, one soldier, a most peculiar one at that, may have been mythologized by Michael Blake in the bestselling novel and Academy Award-winning movie *Dances With Wolves*. Blake tells the story of a Civil War soldier, John Dunbar, who is assigned to an abandoned outpost on the Great Plains. He learns to appreciate and eventually live with the surrounding Native Americans. Dunbar becomes so involved with Indian culture that he eats their food, hunts their buffalo and speaks their language. Although the author claims on the back of the novel's title page that "all the characters in this book are fictitious, and any resemblance to persons living or dead is purely coincidental," an actual Civil War soldier from Hadley, also named John Dunbar, lived with the American Indians and may have provided a model for the author.

Both the real life John Brown Dunbar and his father, Reverend John Dunbar, involved themselves with the Pawnees in the new Nebraska territory. Two years after the father graduated from Williams College in 1832, he went west to serve as a Presbyterian missionary. Writing articles for the *Missionary Herald* in 1834, he describes life among the Pawnees. He details a buffalo hunt from the sighting and killing of the animal to the feasting in the village that follows. His son John Brown Dunbar was born in Bellevue (Omaha), Nebraska, on 3 April 1843 and grew up among the Pawnees. The young man returned to his mother's home town, Hadley, and lived on West Street with his relatives, the Smiths. After graduating from Hopkins Academy (Joseph Hooker's school), he attended Amherst College from 1860-1863. The four mile walk was nothing to a man used to the endless prairie. He enjoyed college life, joining Psi Upsilon fraternity and the Athenian academic group. But in 1863 he withdrew in order to enlist in the 52nd Massachusetts Volunteer Infantry Regiment. Once his nine month enlistment was up, the 6'1" 151 pounder reenlisted with the 16th Massachusetts Light Artillery and served until 27 June 1865. After Dunbar graduated from Amherst (BA, 1865; MA, 1867), he taught Greek and Latin in Vermont, White Plains, New York, and, from 1870-1878, Omaha, Nebraska. At Washburn University he also served as the university librarian.[107] So far, the facts seem to picture a patriotic, rather scholarly person who would never be played on screen by Kevin Costner.

But John Brown Dunbar's real life claim to fame came not from his classroom behavior. He was an expert on the Pawnees. He wrote long essays about their life, a way fading fast in 1880. With admiration he tells of their history, domestic customs and generous behavior. His explanation of their language in a book by the noted Greenfield, Massachusetts, anthropologist George Bird Grinnell is introduced by a picture of a brave using sign language to identify himself: he holds both hands to the sides of his head and raises the first two fingers like wolves' ears, the universal symbol of the Pawnees. In a lengthy history of white men in Kansas, Dunbar comes as close as ever to hinting that his experience had not been all scholarly. "Once my life was saved by a Pawnee," he wrote, "and I still bear the mark of another who meant last things when he gave the blow."[108] In all his writing, he remains sympathetic because "they seem destined to pass away, and leave no special impress."[109]

Blake's novel naturally diverges from these biographical facts. In it, the hero marries a woman in the tribe who had been kidnapped years before from her white parents; John Brown Dunbar married Alida Cook, who does not seem to have been removed from her parents in Topeka. In the book, the Comanches are John Dunbar's people and he helps them defeat the rascally Pawnee raiders. The movie was filmed near Pierre, South Dakota, and the actors speak Lakota (Sioux), but the villains are still Pawnee.[110] In both of Michael Blake's versions, the Pawnees ("the most terrible of all the tribes"[111]) kill the wagon driver who took Dunbar to his isolated post, murder the white girl's father because he won't give them whisky and try to steal horses from the "good" Indians. Also, Blake's main character seems to have been a doer rather than an intellectual; he was an officer and is said to have suffered a severe foot wound, three facts that separate him from the Hadley Dunbar. Mr. Ron Benson, a descendant of the real life soldier-scholar, sent me a tape of the Alan King radio show on which Michael Blake again claimed the story was made up from much reading: "I'd been reading ... particularly western history ... absolutely thrilling and inspiring."[112] Michael Blake elsewhere asserted that he ran across the name of a sergeant Dunbar in enlistment rolls for Kansas.[113]

Despite these contrary data, circumstantial evidence suggests that Blake, the well-read author, brilliantly combined the lives of the two historical Dunbar men and gave fame to a Hadley man. First, the Librarian at the Kansas State Historical Society kindly told me that there was only one Kansan named John Dunbar in the Civil War, but this man was not a sergeant nor did he have any obvious connection to Indians.[114] How many soldiers-who-were-Indian-authorities can there have been?

So far as the different facts, authors always take hints from many places and recombine them. It doesn't seem crucial what tribe, Comanche or Lakota/Sioux, Blake finally chose as his Indians, so John Brown Dunbar's connection with the Pawnee is likewise not crucial. The story of a white girl taken from her parents, married to an Indian brave and retaken by whites sounds incredible, but it also is true. In May 1836 the Comanches kidnapped Cynthia Ann Parker, a nine year old living in northern Texas. After bearing two sons and a daughter to Peta Nocona, she was recaptured in 1860 by government Indian hunters and taken to her father. Although the whites welcomed her, she tried to return to her new people and, failing, starved herself to death in 1864. Even closer to Blake's supposed invention Stands With a Fist is probably the real life Rachel Parker Plummer. This feisty captive, also abducted by Comanches from Parker's Fort, Texas, in 1836, laid low the squaws who had been tormenting her just as did Blake's character.[115]

So it seems possible that the Dunbars, well known experts on Native American lore, may have inspired Michael Blake and given an even longer life to one Hadley soldier.[116]

Chapter Six

Hadley, Post War

In 1865, four years after the war started, Hadley had not really changed in economy, social structure or population. The nimble hands of Canadians still assembled brooms, although Yankees owned the shops. While Hadley continued to hold the corner on the broom industry, tobacco was becoming a more profitable enterprise. No one seemed to notice the increased percentage of foreign-born townspeople: in 1860 it had been only 14.6%; in 1865 it rose to 26.1%; and by 1870 it had shot up to 31.5%.[117] Clichéd misinformation persisted, however. If the newspaper mentioned the Irish, for example, it neglected their vital roles in the economy and merely poked fun at their drunken ways: they overturned sleighs when driving too fast, the newspaper claimed, or tore patches of hair from their wives' heads "as large as the bottom of a tea cup."[118]

Joseph Hooker and John Dunbar choose never to return. Other men, like Daniel H. Bartlett, had been awakened to a world outside the limits of the village. Bartlett, born in Hadley during 1836, served with H/52 as a nurse during his tour. Appointed on a scientific expedition to Africa in October 1889, he may not have come home.[119] J. Howard Jewett, too, grew up as a result of his experiences. He had been only 18 when he joined C/10. Overcoming typhoid fever, he rose to

2nd Lieutenant. After the war, he wrote "some twenty or more volumes of story-books for children; also some patriotic and army verse." By 1907 he was living permanently in New York and a member of the Authors' Club.[120]

No one knows why these men decided to keep moving or to come home. When H. Clement Russell returned to Hadley, there were no elaborate parades or services. Not even one monument was erected. The veterans were expected to reenter immediately the life they had postponed when they left to fight. Perhaps townspeople

Figure 11: Picture from Alfred S. Roe, *The Tenth Regiment Massachusetts Infantry 1861-1864* (Springfield: Tenth Regiment Veterans Association, 1900) 369.

John Howard Jewett (1843-1925), a native of Hadley, was 18 when he joined the Tenth Massachusetts Infantry as a private. Listed as a clerk in civilian life, he rose to the rank of lieutenant before being discharged on 11 July 1864. After the war, he became a successful editor and business manager with *The Holyoke Transcript*, *The Worcester Gazette*, *The Profession* and *The Craftsman*. Then he turned to writing children's stories. His obituary in *The New York Times* (19 September 1925, page 15) summarized Jewett's career: "His 'Bunny Stories' appeared in 1900 and were followed by a long series of juvenile books, including five volumes of 'Christmas Stocking Stories,' ten volumes of 'Little Mother Stories,' and four volumes of 'Grandmother Goose Stories.'"

never thought twice about having their boys take up their familiar chores; they might have sensed that such routines were all that they could now share with men who had seen such horror. One soldier from New Hampshire recalled that the day after he got home from the war, he was out in the fields picking up hay. He thought that it seemed like he was gone for only three days, not three years.[121]

Soldiers returning to Hadley after the war had an advantage. They did not need to fear change, rejection, unemployment or poverty like those who returned to cities like Boston. There was

Figure 12: "The Story of a Life in Rebel Prisons" *Harper's Weekly* 9. 426 (25 February 1865) 120-21.

The tradition of telling tales to the family in front of a large fireplace took on a bitter-sweet tone. As usual, the older members sit nearest the warmth; but what they heard must have chilled their hearts. Conditions in all prisons were appalling. H. Clement Russell survived Belle Isle, but many other captives, blue and gray, did not. Until the atrocity pictures became widespread, however, there seemed to be a possible happy ending if one were captured. A. R. Waud portrayed beaming "Released Prisoners Returning to the Camp of the Thirty-First Regiment New York Volunteers ... from Richmond, Virginia," seemingly none the worse for their trauma (*Harper's Weekly* 6.266 [1 February 1862] 77).

no nervousness about losing a job. Many men, like Truman Meekins and Clement Russell, returned and took active parts not only on their family farms but also as fire marshal, town surveyor and juror.

The war began as one more step toward perfecting our admirable country. Not many months before its outbreak, Reverend W. H. Beaman gave a Thanksgiving sermon in North Hadley, admitting that although the world had not yet quite turned swords into plowshares in 1853, local families "with cheerful faces ... exhibit the results of their ... useful industry."[122] A second sermon preached by Reverend Beaman at the same church in 1884 reminded the congregation that battle had forced everyone to qualify this optimism with "sorrow that some loved ones would not return."[123]

Hadley remembered those who did not return. For years, the grade school bore the name Joseph P. Hooker Elementary school. Every Memorial Day, Cub Scouts and local musicians parade to decorate graves of men like Aaron Scott in North Hadley Cemetery, Henry Dunakin in West Street Cemetery, Charles, Daniel and Henry Howard in Mount Warner Cemetery, Charles Lyman in Hockanum Road Cemetery and H. Clement Russell in Russellville Cemetery. And if the evidence is correct, both the town and the nation remember one soldier from Hadley because of *Dances With Wolves*.

Elsewhere interments ranged from hasty to grandiose. Although Hadley lacks a statue of an ever-vigilant soldier on a pillar, we can still look at the markers in our cemeteries and call to mind these young men who bravely marched to see the elephant.

Appendices

HADLEY RESIDENTS BORN OUTSIDE MASSACHUSETTS

	1860 CENSUS	1865 ABSTRACT	1870 CENSUS
IRELAND	202		256
CANADA	90		202
NEW YORK	-		42
VERMONT	4		30
NEW HAMPSHIRE	11		25
CONNECTICUT	12		24
ENGLAND	1		14
PENNSYLVANIA	-		6
OHIO	-		4
MAINE	5		4
SAXONY	-		4
PRUSSIA	-		4
ILLINOIS	-		2
WISCONSIN	-		2
IOWA	-		2
RHODE ISLAND	1		2
MICHIGAN	-		1
HESSE DARMSTADT	-		1
AZORES ISLANDS	-		1
TOTAL BORN OUTSIDE MASS	**326**	**587**	**626**
TOTAL POPULATION	**2230**	**2246**	**2301**
% BORN OUTSIDE	**14.6%**	**26.1%**	**31.5%**

CASUALTIES

YEAR	WOUNDED	DIED	DISCHARGED FOR DISABILITY	IMPRISONED	DESERTED
1861 61 enlisted	0	0	0	0	1
1862 74 enlisted	3	4	8	3	1
1863 22*	2	9	7	2	4 *all drafted*
1864 47**	26	20	6	10	16 *credited to Hadley*
1865 15**	1	3	6	-	2
TOTAL	32	36	27	23	24

* 15 enlisted, 7 drafted
**Not all Hadley, but many paid by Hadley men to fill quota

	%
TOTAL ENLISTED, DRAFTED AND ACCOUNTED FOR	21
WOUNDED	15
DIED	17
DISCHARGED FOR DISABILITY	12
IMPRISONED	10
DESERTED	11
WOUNDED OR DIED	32
WOUNDED, DIED, DISCHARGED FOR DISABILITY OR IMPRISONED	54

SOURCES AND SYMBOLS

SOURCES	SYMBOLS
Names originally copied from Civil War Plaque, Historical Room, Goodwin Memorial Library, Hadley	∧
1860 U. S. Census.	*
Hadley Records, vol. 4: Elections, Town Meetings, Militia Lists, Highway (3/30/1857 - 12/1/1882). Town Hall, Hadley	>
Massachusetts Soldiers. Sailors. and Marines in the Civil War	•
Record of the Massachusetts Volunteers. 1861-1865	#
Record of Soldiers and Officers in the Military Service ("The Rebellion Book"). Town Hall, Hadley.	<
Grave marker at North Hadley Cemetery.	+
Grave marker at Old Hadley Cemetery.	-
Grave marker at Russellville Cemetery.	~
Grave marker at Mount Warner Cemetery.	=
Grave marker at Hockanum Road Cemetery.	I
Other Sources.	(numbered)

NAME, AGE, OCCUPATION, MARITAL STATUS, ORIGIN, RACE OF MEN CREDITED TO HADLEY IN THE CIVIL WAR

NAME	AGE (1860) BIRTH DATE	OCCUPATION	MARRIED	ORIGIN (if not Hadley) OR RACE
William E. Babbett				
William Baldwin		blacksmith^		
Henry Barber		laborer^		Black^
Daniel Barrett		saddler^		
Dwight Barrett<		wheelwright^	no<	Belchertown^
Daniel H. Bartlett		broom maker	no<	
Estus Bartlett		soldier^		
Charles H. Barton		butcher (^ 4.852)		Amherst^
William Baxter		brass finisher^		
Charles O. Beals		broom maker> farmer^		
John G. Beals		wire maker^ farmer^	no<	
Edwin D. Beaman	11.10.42<	farmer^ <	no<	
John W. Beaman	12.28.45<	student^	no<	
Joseph C. Bell		teamster^		
Leander Bellville, Jr.		broom maker^		
Charles H. Belmont		sailor^		Montreal^
Nazar Benoit		broom maker^	no<	Canada<
Alfred A. Bicknell		operative^		Providence, RI^
Elisha Bigelow		sailor^		Connecticut^
Theodore S. Billings	42 (7*) 1. 21.18<	painter* music teacher^<	yes*	
Thomas Black				
George A. Boice		shoe maker^	yes<	Spencer<

NAME	AGE (1860) BIRTH DATE	OCCUPATION	MARRIED	ORIGIN (if not Hadley) OR RACE
Hiram M. Bolton		farmer^	no<	? Ashulet, NH<
Charles L. Brown		farmer^		
Robert Brown (+)	14+			
Lyman P. Bullard	2.17.39<	farmer^ <		? Ashulet, NH<
Louis Burdette		broom maker^		
Leander Bushman		broom maker^	yes<	Canada<
Elijah Carter	7.5.36<	farmer^ <	yes<	Northfield^ Canada <
Nelson Carter		painter^		
William A. Champney<				
Albert T. Chapin		painter^		
Charles W. Clark	20 (31*) 10.25.39<	farmer*<		Ireland*
Edwin R. Clark		clerk^		Res Boston. Credit Hadley
Irving R. Clark<		farmer^		
John C. Clark	4.23.38<	farmer> broom maker^	no><	
Joseph H. Clark		clerk^		Res Boston. Credit Hadley
Louis Clonette		broom maker^		
William Cockley		blacksmith^		Res Boston. Credit Hadley
Malachi Coggins		laborer^	yes*<	Leverett<
Henry [C. +^] Comins	23 (9*)	farmer*^		
Joseph Concklin		laborer^		Rondout, NY. Credit Hadley
William Connor		pattern maker^		Greenfield, MA^
Eleazer Cook		farmer^		

NAME	AGE (1860) BIRTH DATE	OCCUPATION	MARRIED	ORIGIN (if not Hadley) OR RACE
Frederick L. Cook				
Rufus A. Cook	18 (44*) 3.21.41<	farmer*	no*	
S. Parsons Cook	27 (39*) 3.4.34<	farmer*^<	yes<	
Alfred L. Cook(e^)	12.1.36<	farmer^<	no<	
Alexander Costello		architect'^		Res New York. Credit Hadley^
John Cowan		laborer^	no	Jersey City, NJ. Credit Hadley^
Marshall A. Cowles		farmer^		
Rollin Cowles	3.4.35<	farmer^	yes<	
Silas Cowles	18 (15*) 5.4.41<	farmer*	no<	
Edward Crabtree<	4.24.?48<	farmer<	no<	Canada<
Howard Crabtree				
George M. Crabtree	12.1.45<	farmer^ broom maker<	no<	
George M. Crafts	25+ 5.16.35<	potter> broom maker^	yes<	Res Whately^ ? W. Troy, NY<
Richard Curtis		laborer^		Res Northampton ^
William Darling		teamster^		Toronto, CAN^
Sidney Davis<		mechanic^		Res No'hampton^ Born in Hadley<
William J. Demerritt		clerk^		Res Boston
Augustus E. Dickinson		farmer^		
Charles F. Dickinson	9.3.42<	lumberman^ broom maker<	no<	
Daniel O. Dickinson		student>^	no<	Res Waukegan, IL. Credit Hadley

NAME	AGE (1860) BIRTH DATE	OCCUPATION	MARRIED	ORIGIN (if not Hadley) OR RACE
Levi P. Dickinson (1)		carpenter^		Res Amherst^
Luther W. Dickinson				
James Doody (2)		farmer^		Res Holyoke^
Andrew J. Doolittle (3)		farmer^		Res Hinsdale, NH^
Rodney D. Doolittle		farmer^		Res Hinsdale, NH^
Henry Dunakin		mechanic'^		
Henry A. Dunakin	7.13.37<	broom maker^		
John B. Dunbar		student^		Reen from Seward, KS^
Baldwin Edwards (Balum on plaque)		farmer^		Hawley. (? Hadley)
Franklin Elwell		shoemaker^		
Charles Elwell	28 (45*)	laborer* mechanic^	yes<	
Joseph G. Elwell		mariner^		Res Rockport^
Charles S. Enderton		farmer^		
Henry J. Fales	26 (7*) -.-.33<	laborer* brush maker^	yes ?*<	Res Pelham<
Edgar B. Felton		farmer^		
John Fisher	4.14.32<	broom maker^<	no<	Canada<
James Forsyth	35 (14*)	laborer* mechanic^	yes*	England*
John Franklin		broom maker^		
Francis D. Gleason		farmer^		
William A. Govern		soap maker^		
Charles H. Graham		mechanic^		Res Newark, NJ. Credit Hadley
Edwin E. Gray	16 (33*) 8.24.43<	painter>	no<	Res Prescott<

NAME	AGE (1860) BIRTH DATE	OCCUPATION	MARRIED	ORIGIN (if not Hadley) OR RACE
Joseph Gray		soap maker^ mechanic^		
Joseph L. Greeley		farmer^		Res Temple, NH
John Haggerty, Jr.<		farmer~<		Res Springfield< Born Ireland<
Augustus Harrington				
Patrick E. Hayes				
Peter P. Hayes		machinist^		Res Boston
James W. Hayden<	6.-.40<	mechanic^	no<	
William H. Hayward	27 (34*)	merchant* manufacturer^	yes*	
Henry H. Hemenway	19 (1*) 12.6.40<	laborer* farmer^	yes*	Res Leverett<
Clarence P. Hewitt	20 (51*)	farm laborer*^	no*	
Luman W. Hibbard	24 (10*) 12.24.35<	farmer*	yes*	
Willard Hibbard	48 (2*) 2.3.12<	farmer*	yes*	
Charles Hilger		cook^ broom maker		Res Boston.^ Credit Hadley
Charles D. Hodge	11.15.25<	farmer^<		
John F. Hodge	10.3.36<	laborer^ farmer<		
Samuel Hodge	26 (23*) 9.24.35<	farmer*^		
William H. Hodge	7.24.41<	farmer^	no<	
Sewal B. Holbrook		farmer^ (4)		Credit Milford ^
Albert O. Holley				
Lewis B. Hooker	11.18.35<	broom maker^<		
Charles T. Howard	4.4.37<	laborer^		Res Amherst<
Daniel S. Howard	21 (15*)	farmer* carpenter^	no*	

NAME	AGE (1860) BIRTH DATE	OCCUPATION	MARRIED	ORIGIN (if not Hadley) OR RACE
Henry E. Howard	17 (17*)	farmer*	no*	
Oscar R. Hubbard	2.20.40<	broom maker<	no<	Res Hubbardston <
James W. Irving				
Abraham Jannotte	9.28.34<	broom maker^	yes<	Canada<
Francis N. Jennings (4)	17 (3)	farmer^ (4)	no<	
J. Howard Jewett	1.19.43<	clerk^		Black (4)
Edward Johnson<	12.22.38<	farmer<		
George [A. 5] Johnson		sailor^		Pictou, NS, Credit Hadley
Herbert F. Johnson	7.13.37<	farmer^	no<	
George N. Jones	24 (24*) 3.29.36<	farmer*^<		
David Jordan		clerk^		Chelsea^
Patrick Kane				
Louis G. Keene		machinist^		South Boston^
Samuel B. Kehew		cooper^		Salem. Credit Hadley^
John Kelly (Kelley on plaque)		laborer^		Pittsfield^
Silas Dwight Kellogg		farmer^	yes<	
Frederick B. Kentfield	12.-.45<	farmer^	no<	
John King		laborer^		
Joseph Labell<				
Louis Lancour	3.18.28<	laborer^ broom maker<	yes<	Canada<
Jacob Larivere		farmer^	no<	Canada<
Thomas Laurie				
William F. Leggett		farmer^		Res West Haven, VT^

NAME	AGE (1860) BIRTH DATE	OCCUPATION	MARRIED	ORIGIN (if not Hadley) OR RACE
Louis Lizard (Ligard #2.789)		broom maker^		St. Michael, Canada
Benjamin Lumbard, Jr		seaman^	no<	
Charles A. Lyman	19 (51*) 2.1.41<	farmer*^		
Warren J. Lyman		wheelwright^		
Rufus D. Marsh	16 (+) 6.28.45<	laborer^ farmer<		
William D. Maurer				
Patrick McCabe		laborer^		Res Springfield (^3.140) Res Boston (^3.184)
Michael McNalley (McNulley on plaque)		cabinet maker^		Boston^
Charles McQuade				
Truman Meekins	1.10.25<	farmer^ broom mfgr<		Res Whately<
Frederick Meyer		artist^		Hoboken, NJ^
George Miller		clerk^		Williamsburg, LI, NY ^
John Miller		miller>	yes>	
John D. Miller	26 (7*) 9.12.33<	farm laborer* broom maker^	no*	
Francis Mousen	1.17.39<	laborer< broom maker<	yes<	Canada<
Lotes C. Montague		farmer^		
Merrick Montague (~)	26 (~)	carpenter^		Res Sunderland^
William R. Montague	22 (+) 11. 23. 38<	farmer^	no<	
Charles D. Moody				

NAME	AGE (1860) BIRTH DATE	OCCUPATION	MARRIED	ORIGIN (if not Hadley) OR RACE
William C. Morrill<		farmer^		Res Northampton ^
Michael Morrison				
Martin A. Munroe				Res Boston^
John Murphy				
Joseph Nado		broom maker^		Res Montreal'^
George W. Nash	15 (27*) 5.10.45<	farmer*<	no*	
Jay E. Nash	3.29.43<	farmer^	yes<	
Joseph Neddeau< NIDO^		laborer^		Res Northampton
Harlow Newton		machinist^		Res South Hadley
Myron Newton			yes	
John Norton				
Thomas Nugent [Tom *]	30 (14*)	laborer* mechanic^		Ireland*
Madison R. Olds		farmer^		
Otto Pappenheim		artist^		Res New York^
Charles A. Parker				
William Pate				Attleboro
Nathan Perkins		farmer^		
William Perkins	39 (3*) 5.17.20+	farmer* mechanic^	no*	Lancaster,< NH*
Edward Phillips		farmer^		
Francis Pilkey	2.11.29<	broom maker^<	yes<	Canada<
E. Henry Potter	22 (45*) 3.2.40<	mason* farmer^	no*	
Richard M. Powers, Jr				

NAME	AGE (1860) BIRTH DATE	OCCUPATION	MARRIED	ORIGIN (if not Hadley) OR RACE
Rodney M. Powers		farmer^		
Simeon E. Preston<		wheelwright^		Amherst^
Joseph Prevo(e ^)	4.15.31<	broom maker^	yes<	Canada<
Frederick S. Prior	17 (45*) 7.21.42<	farmer*^	no*	
Orville W. Prouty (+)	16 (+)	boot click^		Credit Spencer
Edmund Putsch (Pietsch^)		artist^		Credit Hadley
William O. Quinn		laborer		Nova Scotia^
George Reynolds	21 (48*)	laborer* farmer^		
Harvey L. Rhood		farmer^	yes<	
William C. Rodman		operative^	yes (7)	Moodus, CN. Credit Hadley
Joseph Root		laborer^		
Charles L. Russell (~)	22 (~)	farmer^		Sunderland^
Frederick S. Russell	26 (9*) 9.29.34< 1824~ (note years)	operative* farmer<	no*	
H. Clement Russell	15 (12*) 10.8.44	farmer*^	no*	
John F. Russell	20 (12*)	farmer*	no*	
Warren E. Russell		farmer (mv 2.527)^		
Willard A. Russell	23 (12*)	broom maker	no*	
Jacob Rust		farmer^		Res Amherst^
John Sammon		laborer^		
John Scannal				
Aaron Scott (+)	25 (+)			

NAME	AGE (1860) BIRTH DATE	OCCUPATION	MARRIED	ORIGIN (if not Hadley) OR RACE
Rufus P. Scott	30 (3*) 5.1.29<	farmer*^<	yes*<	
Daniel Sculley				
Silas Sebean		farmer^		
Thomas (H.A) Sheppard				Res Boston
Hiram Shumway<		farmer<		
Edwin B. Smith		farmer^		
Frederick H. Smith	16 (45*) 2.9.45<	farmer*^	no*	See also 48*
George M[yron ~] Smith	15 (8*) 5.28.44<	farmer*^<	no*<	
James W. Smith	6. L 38<	farmer< merchant^	yes<	
Joseph F. Smith	17 (45*) 12.9.42<	farmer*^<	no*<	(8)
Lucius D. Smith	18 (44*) 11.22.41<	farmer*^	no*	(9)
Samuel D. Smith	12.10.34<	farmer^	no<	
Joseph O. Spear	40 (7*) 1.14.20<	farmer*^<	yes*<	Res Amherst<
Charles O. Squires	7.27.42<	mechanic> clerk^	yes>	Res Palmer<
Anton Stern		brewer^		New York^
Francis J. Stockbridge	16 (9*) 3.9.44<	farmer*^ <	no*<	
Sylvester L. Stockbridge	18 (9*) 5.22.41<	student>^<	no*	
Charles A. Story	17 (10) 12.30.42<	farmer^< (10)	no< (10)	Black (10) Hudson, NY<
William A. Story (11)	23 (11)	barber^ (11)	no (11)	Black (11)
James Sullivan		carpenter^		Chicopee^ (12)
John Sullivan<		farmer<	no<	

NAME	AGE (1860) BIRTH DATE	OCCUPATION	MARRIED	ORIGIN (if not Hadley) OR RACE
Michael Talbot		farmer^		Res Amherst^
John Taylor				
William Taylor		mason^		Bristol, CT^
Lyman R. Thayer (13)				
Samuel M. Thayer (14)		carpenter^		
Moses Thessier	4.18.43<	broom maker^<		Canada<
Ciliste Thibault (Silas Tebo<)				
Benjamin A. Till	16 (52*)	laborer*^		Black* (15)
Samuel C. Till	15 (16)	broom maker^(16)	no (16)	Black (16)
John Tompkins (no first name on plaque)		laborer^		Buffalo, NY^
Alvin Trim				
John W. Turner		clerk^		Boston^
John Vail	5.3.42<	printer^ farmer<	no<	Ireland<
Alfred Van Horn		broom maker^	no<	
Avery A. Ward	-.12.35<	farmer^	yes<	Res Munson<
Charles Warren		seaman (17)		New York. Credit Hadley
George H. Webber<		farmer<	no<	Res Chicopee^
Lewis W. West	11.27.34<	(law<) student^	no<	
Francis P. Wheeler		farmer^		(18)
Charles H. White	16 (28*) 1.28.44<	farmer* broom maker<	no*<	
Francis M. White	18 (28*)	farmer* broom maker	no*	

NAME	AGE (1860) BIRTH DATE	OCCUPATION	MARRIED	ORIGIN (if not Hadley) OR RACE
Charles H. Wilbur	3.4.38<	farmer< broom maker	no<	
Ebenezer F. Wiley (~)	20 (~)	carpenter		Res Sunderland^
Asa Williams				
George H. Williams	10.15.32<	mechanic^ farmer<		
Isaiah Williams				
Lyman Williams				
John Williams				
Lyman Williams				
Charles Woston		sailor^		Australia^
Orien E. Writer		farmer^		
Joseph Young		broom maker^		

ADDITIONAL SOURCES

1. Levi P. Dickinson served in Company F, 37th Regiment, Massachusetts Volunteer Infantry. Enlisted 30 August 1862, he was "discharged owing to disability caused by sickness" on 17 June 1864. Carpenter & Morehouse, compilers, *The History of the Town of Amherst. Massachusetts. 1731-1896* (Amherst: Carpenter & Morehouse, 1896), 508. This fact contradicts the optimistic note in the *Hampshire Gazette and Northampton Courier* 10 March 1863: 1, 5 concerning the condition of men at Fredericksburg, Virginia: "There are now in the hospital between thirty and forty, none are considered so sick as Levi Dickinson of North Hadley, but he is considered on the improve."

2. James Doody, although listed as a resident of Holyoke in *Massachusetts Soldiers* 4:610, is included among the Hadley volunteers in the *Hampshire Gazette,* 11 November 1863: 2, 5. J. F. Moors, *History of the Fifty-Second Regiment Massachusetts Volunteers* (Boston: George H. Ellis, 1893) xxxviii, says he was born in Ireland and enlisted in Hadley.

3. Andrew J. Doolittle, although listed as a resident of Hinsdale, NH, in *Massachusetts Soldiers* 4:610, is included among the Hadley volunteers in the *Hampshire Gazette,* 11 November 1863: 2, 5.

4. Francis N. Jennings served in Company H, 54th Regiment, Massachusetts Infantry. Seventeen years old when he enlisted in Hadley on 23 November 1863, he was a single farmer. Ended his service in Boston on 20 August 1865 and received a state bonus of $325. Luis F. Emilio, *History of the Fifty-Fourth Regiment of the Massachusetts Volunteer Infantry.* 2nd edition (Boston: Boston Book Company, 1894) 375.

5. George A. Johnson was awarded a monthly pension of $10 per month for a back injury. Date of original award not given. *List of Pensioners on the Roll. January 1 1883* (Baltimore: Genealogical Publishing Company, 1970) 1:369. This may be the same man.

6. Myron Newton, son of John Newton, died at Hartsville, Tennessee, while serving with Company G, 104 Illinois Volunteers. According to the notice in the *Hampshire Gazette*, 30 December 1862: 2, 8. He was 26, married and left a brother.

7. William C. Rodman was married. George MacNamara, *The History of the Ninth Regiment Massachusetts Volunteer Infantry Second Brigade. First Division. Fifth Army Corps. Army of the Potomac June. 1861-June. 1864* (Boston: E. B. Stillings, 1899) 441.

8. Joseph F. Smith was awarded a pension of $6 per month for a "rheum. arm." Date of original award not given. *List of Pensioners*, 369.

9. Lucius D. Smith was awarded a pension on 17 March 1882 of $2 per month for an injury to his right leg. *List of Pensioners*, 369.

10. Charles Story served in Company B, 54th Regiment, Massachusetts Infantry. Twenty years old when he enlisted in Hadley on 18 July 1863, he was a single farmer. Ended his service 20 August 1865 in Boston. Emilio, *History*, 348.

11. William Story served in Company B, 54th Regiment, Massachusetts Infantry. 26 years old when he enlisted in Hadley on 2 December 1863, he was a single barber. Ended his service on 20 August 1865 in Boston and received a state bounty of $325. Emilio, *History*, 348.

12. James Sullivan is mentioned as one of the Hadley casualties at Newbern in the *Hampshire Gazette*, 25 March 1862: 1, 6. Because Hadley had rapidly filled its quota for 1861, it is possible that Sullivan fibbed about his place of residence.

13. Lyman R. Thayer, Hadley, is said to have been in G/27th briefly. Enlisted 7.28.62; "discharged owing to disability" on 2.8.63. (Carpenter & Morehouse, *History*, 507.)

There is no record of Lyman R. Thayer in *Massachusetts Soldiers*, but Lyman Thayer, an 18-year-old farmer from Amherst, enlisted and mustered 7.24.62. This man was also discharged for disability on 10.22.62. (*MSS* 3:187).

14. Samuel M. Thayer served in Company F, 37th Regiment, Massachusetts Infantry. Enlisted 30 August 1862, he was "discharged owing to disability caused by sickness" on 30 March 1863. Carpenter & Morehouse, *History*, 509. *MSS* 3:802 lists Thayer as an Amherst resident but the dates are almost identical.

15. Benjamin Till served in Company I, 54th Regiment, Massachusetts Infantry. Sixteen years old when he enlisted in Hadley on 30 November 1863, he was a single laborer. Died 9 April 1864 at Jacksonville, Florida. Emilio, *History*, 382.

16. Samuel Till served in Company C, 54th Regiment, Massachusetts Infantry. Eighteen years old when he enlisted in Hadley on 11 December 1863, he was a single broom maker. Ended his service on 20 December 1865 in Boston and received a state bounty of $325. Emilio, *History*, 353.

17. Charles Warren is listed in Alfred S. Roe, *The Twenty-Fourth Regiment Massachusetts Volunteers 1861-1866* (Worcester, MA: Twenty-Fourth Veteran Association, 1907) 559.

18. Francis P. Wheeler was awarded a pension of $4 per month for the loss of his thumb. Date of original award not given. *List of Pensioners*, 369.

ABBREVIATIONS FOR MILITARY UNITS

Bat	Battery
IV	Illinois Volunteer Infantry
KSCAV	Kansas Cavalry
MI	Massachusetts Infantry
MVCav	Massachusetts Volunteer Cavalry
MVHA	Massachusetts Volunteer Heavy Artillery
MVI	Massachusett's Volunteer Infantry
MVLA	Massachusetts Volunteers Light Artillery
MVM	Massachusetts Volunteer Militia (90 days' service)
NCHA	North Carolina Heavy Artillery
NEVC	New England Volunteer Cavalry
RI	Inf Rhode Island Infantry
USArt	United States Artillery (Regular Army)
USCI	United States Colored Infantry
USInf	United States Infantry (Regular Army)
VLC	Veteran Reserve Corps (formerly the Invalid Corps)

ABBREVIATIONS FOR SERVICE HISTORIES

D	Died
Disab	Disability
Dis	Discharged
Exch	Exchanged
Must	Mustered out
Pris	Prisoner
Reen	Reenlisted
Trans	Transferred
Wnd	Wounded

Keyed To *Massachusetts Soldiers, Sailors, And Marines In The Civil War*

9 Vols. Boston: Wright & Potter, 1932-1937.
(Other Sources Indicated By Footnote)

NAME	MSS vol. p	AGE/ MUSTER IN DATE	UNIT	SERVICE HISTORY
William E. Babbett				
William Baldwin	6.162	21/9.18.61	E/1 MVCav	Dis 9.17.64
Henry Barber	7.321	20/5.25.64	A/43 USCI	Must 10.20.65
Daniel Barrett	6.783	23/7.6.64	G/3 USInf	Deserted 9.13.64
Dwight Barrett<	3.144	23/10.19.61	D/27	D 6.2.64, Cold Harbor, VA
Daniel H. Bartlett	4.609	26/10. 11. 62	H/52	Must 8.14.63
Estus Bartlett	6.783	31/7.9.64	C/USInf	Deserted 9.12.64. Prior service K/4USArt
Charles H. Barton	3.144	24/9.7.61	D/27	Wnd 3.14.62, Newbern, NC. Dis for wounds 7.29.62
	4.852	27/4.6.64	G/57	Pris 3.25.65, Ft. Stedman, VA. Exch 3.29.65. Must 7.30.65
William Baxter	6.783	24/7.7.64	G/3 USInf	Deserted 9.13.64
Charles O. Beals	4.609	18/10.11. 62	H/52	Must 8.14.63
John G. Beals	3.798	21/8.30.62	F/37	D of disease 2.22.63, Washington
Edwin D. Beaman	3.798	19/8.30.62	F/37	Dis for disab 3.21.64.
John W. Beaman	5.358	18/1. 4. 64	2 Bat/ MVLA	Must 6.5.65, Washington
Joseph C. Bell	3.144	25/10.7.61	D/27	Dis for disab 9.11.62, Newbern, NC

NAME	MSS vol. p	AGE/ MUSTER IN DATE	UNIT	SERVICE HISTORY
Leander Bellville, Jr	4.609	18/11. 4.62	H/52	Wnd in arm 6.17.63, Port Hudson, LA Must 8.14.63
Charles H. Belmont	2.488	21/8.1. 63	unassigned	Deserted 8.14.63. Drafted.
Nazar Benoit	5.358	18/1.4.64	2 Bat/ MVLA	D of disease 4.18.64, New Orleans
Alfred A. Bicknell	3.22	21/1. 26. 65	D/25	Must 7.13.65
Elisha Bigelow	2.67	26/8.26.63	D/22	Pris 5.23.64, North Anna River,VA. D of disease 8.11.64, Andersonville, VA
Theodore S. Billings	3.144	43/10.14.61	D/27	Dis 11.1.64, Newbern, NC
Thomas Black				
George A. Boice	3.163	39/10.17.61	G/27	Reen 11.25.63. Pris 5.16.62,Drury's Bluff, VA. D of disease 10.10.64 (9.8.64<), Andersonville
Hiram M. Bolton	4.609	20/10.11.62	H/52	D of disease 8.18.63, Mound City Hospital<, Cairo, IL
Charles L. Brown	4.609	18/10.11.62	H/52	D of disease 5.15.63, hospital, Baton Rouge, LA
Robert Brown				
Lyman P. Bullard	4.609	23/ 10.11. 62	H/52	Dis 9.5.63
Louis Burdette	6.217	28/1.14.64	M/l MVC	Must out of D/1 MVC 6.29.65

NAME	MSS vol. p	AGE/ MUSTER IN DATE	UNIT	SERVICE HISTORY
Leander Bushman	5.359	21/1. 4. 64	2 Bat/ MVLA	Drowned 12.64 (4.18.64<) when steamer North America sank
Elijah Carter	3.137	24/9.30.61 10.10.61<	C/27	Reen as Cpl 11.25.63. Pris 5.16.64 Drury's Bluff, VA. Exchd 11.17.64. Sgt 2.6.65. Must 6.26.65
Nelson Carter	6.191	23/12.5.63	1/1 MVCav	Wnd 5.5.64, Todd's Tavern, VA. Pris. D of disease 12.12.64, Florence, SC
William A. Champney<	3.798	19/8.30.62	F/37	Hospital Steward 10.7.62.Dis 6.21.65
Albert T. Chapin	3.169	24/10.1. 61	H/27	Dis for disab 5.24.62, Newbern, NC
Charles W. Clark	4.609	22/10.11.62	H/52	D of typhoid fever 4.20.63,hospital, Baton Rouge, LA
Edwin R. Clark	6.52	19/8.18.64	K/4 MVHA	Must 6.17.65
Irving R. Clark<	3.169	21/9.20.61	H/27	Reen 1.1.64. Cpl 4.5.64. Pris 5.16.64, Drury's Bluff,VA. Exch 3.10.65. Must 6.9.65
John C. Clark	1.696	23/6.21.61	C/10	Cpl. Wnd 5.12.64, Spottsylvania, VA. D 5.21.64, White House Landing, VA
Joseph H. Clark	6.5	18/8.16.64	K/MVHA	Cpl 4.15.65. Must 6.17.65

NAME	MSS vol. p	AGE/ MUSTER IN DATE	UNIT	SERVICE HISTORY
Louis Clonette	6.218	19/1.14.64	M/1 MVCav	Sent to D 5.64, Camp Stoneman, DC Deserted
William Cockley	2.806	25/1. 21. 65	F/24	Must 1. 20.86
Malachi Coggins	5.842	31/8.25.64	M/3 MVHA	Must 6.17.65
Henry C. Comins	4.61	25/10.11. 62	H/52	Must 8.14.63
Joseph Concklin	1.657	21/8.21.63	G/9	Deserted 10.29.63. Drafted
William Connor	1.651	21/8.20.63	F/9	Deserted 2.10.64 from hospital Philadelphia. Drafted
Eleazer Cook	4.61	26/10.11.62	H/52	Wnd in arm 6.14.63, Port Hudson, LA Must 8.14.63
Frederick L. Cook	7.151			
Rufus A. Cook, Cpl	3.145	20/9.20.61	D/27	D of diarrhea 2.25.63, Chester General Hospital<, Newbern, NC
S. Parsons Cook	4.61	29/10.11. 62	H/52	Must 8.14.63
Alfred L. Cook(e^)	4.61	25/10.11.62	H/52	Must 8.14.63
Alexander Costello	6.414	27/7.8.64	-/3 MVCav	Deserted on route
John Cowan	1.657	22/8.21. 63	G/9	Deserted 10.29.63, Warrenton, VA. Drafted
Marshall A. Cowles	3.145	20/9.20.61	D/27	Wnd 6.2.64, Cold Harbor, VA. D of disease 6.19.65, Newbern, NC
Rollin Cowles	3.145	27/8.1.62	D/27	D 6.2.64, Cold Harbor, VA

NAME	MSS vol. p	AGE/ MUSTER IN DATE	UNIT	SERVICE HISTORY
Silas Cowles	3.145	20/9.20.61	D/27	D 6.16.64, near Petersburg, VA
Edward Crabtree<	6.218	18/1.14.64	M/1 MVCav	Must 6.26.65 from H/1 MVCav
Howard Crabtree				
George M. Crabtree	4.61	19/10.11.62	H/52	Must 8.14.63
	6.218	1.14.64	Gil MVCav	Must 6.26.65
George M. Crafts, Cpl	4.609	27/10.11.62	H/52	Must 8.14.63
Richard Curtis	3.164	18/12.21.63	G/27	Pris 5.16.64. Drury's Bluff, VA. 3.8.65, South Grove, VA. Caught 4.20.65. Must 7.14.65
Sidney Davis<	3.145	25/10.14.61	D/27	Wnd 6.15.64, Petersburg, VA. Must 9.27.64
William J. Demerritt	5.161	20/1.26.65	K/61	Must 7.16.65
Augustus E. Dickinson	4.610	21/10.11.62	H/52	Pris 6.20.62, Libey Prison<, Jackson, LA. End of record
Charles F. Dickinson	4.61	20/10.11.62	H/52	Must 8.14.63
Daniel O. Dickinson	5.36	18/1.4.64	2 Bat/ MVLA	Must 8.11.65 as Cpl
Levi P. Dickinson	3.799	29/8.30.62	F/37	Dis for disab 1.17.64
Luther W. Dickinson	4.61	31/11.19.62	H/52	Must 8.14.63
James Doody	4.61	20/11.4.62	H/52	Must 8.14.63
Andrew J. Doolittle	4.61	24/11. 4.62	H/52	Must 8.14.63
Rodney D. Doolittle	4.61	19/10.11. 62	H/52	Must 8.14.63
Henry Dunakin, 2nd<	3.146	26/9.20.61	D/27	Wnd 3.14.62, Newbern, NC. D 6.18.64, near Petersburg, VA (D 6.2.64, Cold Harbor, VA<)

NAME	MSS vol. p	AGE/ MUSTER IN DATE	UNIT	SERVICE HISTORY
Henry A. Dunakin	1.696	23/6.21. 61	C/10	Reen 12. 21. 63. Trans
	3.805	26/6.20.64	G/37	Trans
	2.515	26/6.19.65	C/20	Must 7.28.65
John B. Dunbar	4.61	21/10.11.62	H/52	Must 8.14.63
	5.548	3.11.64	16 Bat/ MVLA	Must 6.27.65
Baldwin Edwards (1) (Balum on plaque)		25/3.8.65	1 NCArt	
Charles Elwell	3.146	29/9.20.61	D/27	Dis for disab 7.19.62, Newbern, NC
Franklin Elwell	3.146	22/9.20.61	D/27	Wnd 5.9.64, Arrowfield Church, VA. Must 9.27.64 as Sgt
Joseph G. Elwell	5.293	39/12.9.64	25Unatt/ MVI	Must 6.29.65
Charles S. Enderton	4.609	25/10.11.62	H/52	Cpl 10.2.62. Must 8.14.63
Henry J. Fales	3.799	29/8.30.62	F/37	D 4.1.63, White Oak Church, VA
Edgar B. Felton	6.485	19/3.1.64	M/4 MVCav	Must 11.14.65
John Fisher	6.219	22/1.14.64	M/1 MVCav	Must 6.26.65 as 1 Sgt, A/1MVCav
James Forsyth	4.61	34/10.11.62	H/52	Must 8.14.63
John Franklin	4.61	25/11. 4.62	H/52	Must 8.14.63
Francis D. Gleason	3.17	27/10.1.61	H/27	Cpl 4.1. 63. Dis for disab 4.5.64, Julian's Creek, VA
William A. Govern	3.187	29/12.21. 63	unassigned	Rejected 1. 3.64
Charles H. Graham	2.83	23/1. 5. 65	K/24	Dis for disab 5.19.65
Edwin E. Gray	4.609	19/10.11. 62	H/52	Musician. (Drummer<) Must 8.14.63

NAME	MSS vol. p	AGE/ MUSTER IN DATE	UNIT	SERVICE HISTORY
Joseph Gray	3.146	23/10.10.61	D/27	Deserted 10.31.61, Springfield
Joseph L. Greeley	6.524	19/7.13.64	H/5 MVCav	Deserted 6.1.65
Augustus Harrington	2.671	18/9.6.61	D/22	Dis for minority 2.12.62
John Haggerty, Jr.<	2.807	18/9.12.61	F/24	Dis 9.10.64
Patrick E. Hayes				
Peter P. Hayes	6.563	21/1. 2. 65	E/1 MVCav	Must 6.30.65 as Sgt
James W. Hayden<	2.634	21/8.23.61	H/21	Must 8.30.64
William H. Hayward	4.61	29/10.11.62	H/52	Must 8.14.63
Henry H. Hemenway	4.61	21/10.11. 62	H/52	Must 8.14.63
Clarence P. Hewitt	3.17	21/10.1.61	H/27	Must 9.27.64
Luman W. Hibbard	3.147	26/9.20.61	D/27	Must 9.27.64
Willard Hibbard	3.147	45/10.14.61	D/27	Dis for disab 1.1.62, Annapolis
Charles Hilger	4.179	39/9.23.62	G/42	Pris 1.1.63, Galveston, TX Paroled. Must 8.20.63
	5.205	41/5.4.64	7 Unatt MVM	Must 8.5.64
	6.52	41/8.18.64	K/4 MVHA	Must 6.17.65
Charles D. Hodge	3.8	35/8.30.62	F/37	Must 6.21. 65
John F. Hodge	6.151	18/12.24.63	C/1 MVCav	Must 6.29.65
Samuel Hodge	3.8	26/8.30.62	F/37	Must 6.21.65 as Cpl
William H. Hodge	4.61	21/10.11.62	H/52	Must 8.14.63
Sewal B. Holbrook	2.283	20/7.5.64	B/17	Must 7.11. 65
Albert O. Holley				

NAME	MSS vol. p	AGE/ MUSTER IN DATE	UNIT	SERVICE HISTORY
Lewis B. Hooker	4.609	26/10.11.62	H/52	Sgt 10.2.62. Must 8.14.63
Charles T. Howard	3.139	26/1. 2. 64	C/27	Pris 5.16.64, Drury's Bluff, VA. D of disease 9.12.64, Andersonville
Daniel S. Howard	3.147	21/9.20.61	D/27	D of disease 1.1.64, Portsmouth, VA
Henry E. Howard	3.147	21/9.20.61	D/27	D of disease 7.21.62, Newbern, NC
Oscar R. Hubbard	4.61	23/11.19.62	H/52	Must 8.14.63. (2)
James W. Irving (3)		34/12.24.63	unassigned	Rejected 1. 2. 64
Abraham Jannotte	5.363	26/1.25.64	2 Bat/ MVLA	Must 8.11. 65
Francis N. Jennings	4.697	20/10.23.63	H/54	Must 8.20.65
J. Howard Jewett	1.697	18/6.21.61	C/10	Trans 7.8.63. to F/ VRC. Dis 7.11.64
Edward Johnson<		EnI8.1.63<	H/14 KSCav<	
George Johnson	2.831	19/1. 4.65	K/24	Must 1. 20. 66
Herbert F. Johnson	3.17	24/10.2.61	H/27	Must 9.27.64
George N. Jones	3.8	26/8.30.62.	F/37	1 Sgt 9.11.62<. 2 Lt 1.17.63. 1 Lt 12.24.63. Wnd 6.5.64, Cold Harbor. Pris 2.1.65. Capt 3.21. 65<. Trfd 6.19.65 to
	2.582		K/20	Must 7.16.65
David Jordan	6.52	19/8.18.64	K/4 MVHA	Must 6.17.65
Patrick Kane				
Louis G. Keene	6.53	18/8.16.64	K/4 MVHA	Must 6.17.65

NAME	MSS vol. p	AGE/ MUSTER IN DATE	UNIT	SERVICE HISTORY
Samuel B. Kehew	5.587	31/7.5.61	D/1 MVHA	Dis for disab 11.7.62
	7.202	34/7.7.64	C/19 VRC	Must 11.15.65
Silas Dwight Kellogg	4.608	37/10.11. 62	H/52	Sgt 10.2.62. Must 8.14.63
John Kelly (Kelley on plaque)	3.82	21/1.26.65	K/37 K/20 MI	Trans 6.21.65 to Must 6.26.65
Frederick B. Kentfield	3.147	18/2.5.64	D/27	Pris 3.8.65, South West Creek, NC Exch 3.27.65. Must 6.26.65
John King	4.865	21/2.23.64	Jan-57	Deserted 3.18.64, Worcester
Joseph Labell<				
Louis Lancour	5.364	37/1. 4. 64	2 Bat/ MVLA	Must 8.11.65
Jacob Larivere	5.364	23/1. 4. 64	2 Bat/ MVLA	Must 8.11.65
Thomas Laurie				
William F. Leggett	3.8	18/8.30.62	F/37	D 4.6.65, Sailor's (Wilson's<) Creek, VA
Louis Lizard (4)	3.81	18/11. 25.63	H/37	Missing 5.6.64, Wilderness, VA
Benjamin Lumbard	4.611	32/10.11. 62	H/52	Must 8.14.63
Charles A. Lyman	3.171	20/10.1. 61	H/27	Pris 5.16.64, Drury's Bluff, VA Released 4.28.65. Must 5.22.65
Warren J. Lyman	3.8	31/8.30.62	F/37	Dis for disab 5.28.63, White Oak Church, VA
Rufus D. Marsh	5.365	18/1. 4. 64	2 Bat/ MVLA	Dis for disab 3.17.65, New Orleans
William D. Maurer				

NAME	MSS vol. p	AGE/ MUSTER IN DATE	UNIT	SERVICE HISTORY
Patrick McCabe	3.14	43/1. 23. 65	C/27	Dis 6.26.65
Michael McNally (McNulley on plaque)	5,365	21/7.7.64	2 Bat/ MVLA	Must 8.11. 65
Charles McQuade				
Truman Meekins	4.611	37/10.11.62	H/52	Must 7.21.63, Boston
Frederick Meyer	6.417	32/7.8.64	3 Reg/ MVCav	Deserted on route
George Miller	6.417	30/7.8.64	3 Reg/ MVCav	Deserted on route
John Miller				
John D. Miller	3.801	28/8.30.62	F/37	Dis for disab 3.1.64
Francis Mousen	5.366	25/1. 4.64	2 Bat/ MVLA	Must 8.11. 65
Lotes C. Montague	3.495	28/7.18.63	F/32	Must 6.29.65. NB DRAFTED
Merrick Montague	4.607	27/10.11.62	G/52	Dis for disab 4.1.63, Boston
William R. Montague	3.148	22/9.20.61	D/27	1 Sgt 3.8.64. Must 9.27.64
Charles L. Moody (D. on plaque)	3.433	23/9.30.61		false reference. nothing on this page
William C. Morrill<	3.806	21/8.30.62	G/37	2 Lt 11.1.64. Wnd 9.16.64, Winchester, VA. 1 Lt 2.17.65. Brevet Capt 4.6.65. Must 6.21.65 from E/37
Michael Morrison				
Martin A. Munroe	6.5	19/8.18.64		2 Lt 3.21.65. Must 6.17.65
John Murphy				

NAME	MSS vol. p	AGE/ MUSTER IN DATE	UNIT	SERVICE HISTORY
Joseph Nado	3.14	32/1.2.64	C/27	Pris 5.16.64, Drury's Bluff, VA. Exch 3.11.65 Dis for disab 5.15.65, Baltimore
George W. Nash	3.801	17/8.30.62	F/37	Wnd 6.5.64, Cold Harbor, VA. Dis for wounds 4.13.65, Worcester
Jay E. Nash	3.148	18/9.20.61	D/27	Cpl 5.10.63. Reen 11.25.63. Wnd 7.16.64, Petersburgh, VA. Sgt Creek, NC. Exch 3.27.65. Must 6.15.65
Joseph Neddeau< NIDO^	3.433	20/11.24.61	G/31	Must 1.8.65 NIDO
Harlow Newton	3.433	19/12.1. 61	G/31	Reen 2.13.64 as Cpl. Must as Pvt C/31 9.9.65
John Norton				
Myron Newton			G/104 IV	D before 12.30.62. (5)
Thomas Nugent	4.609	27/10.11.62	H/52	Cpl 10.2.62. Must 8.14.63
Madison R. Olds	3.148	21/10.14.61	D/27	Reen 1.1.64. Wnd 6.15.64, Petersburgh, VA. D of wounds 1.27.65, Morehead City, NC
Otto Pappenheim (Paltenheim on plaque)	6.417	27/7.8.64	unassigned /3 MVCav	

NAME	MSS vol. p	AGE/ MUSTER IN DATE	UNIT	SERVICE HISTORY
Charles A. Parker	4.611	22/11.19.62	Aug-52	Deserted 11.22.62, New York
William Pate	6.633	9.4.62	F/7RI Inf	D 6.3.64, Bathesda Church, VA
Nathan Perkins	4.611	29/11.4.62	H/52	D 8.5.63, Mound City, IL
William Perkins	5.608	41/10.11. 62	Aug-52	Capt. 9.5.62. Must 8.20.63
Edward Phillips	3.599	18/12.28.63	B/34	Pris 10.13.64, Cedar Creek, VA. Exch 2.20.65. Trans 6.16.65 to
	2.783		A/24	as Cpl 1.1.66. Must 1.20.66
Francis Pilkey	5.367	35/1. 4. 64	2 Bat/ MVLA	Must 8.11.65
E. Henry Potter	3.148	22/9.12.61	D/27	D 6.3.64, Cold Harbor, VA
Richard M. Powers, Jr.	1.728	20/9.12.61	10-Jan	Dis for disab 10.7.62
Rodney M. Powers	2.635	18/8.5.61	H/21	Dis 10.22.62 to enl in Reg. Army
	7.21	19/10.23.62	USA	Dis 2.25.67
Simeon E. Preston<	3.148	24/9.20.61	D/27	Cpl. Wnd 6.2.64, Cold Harbor, VA. Must 9.27.64 as Sgt
Joseph Prevo(e ^)	5.367	29/1. 4. 64	2 Bat/ MVLA	Must 8.11.65
Frederick S. Prior	3.148	19/9.20.61	D/27	D 6.18.64, Petersburg, VA
Orville W. Prouty	3.615	18/7.31. 62	E/34	Must 6.16.65
Edmund Putsch (Pietsch)	7.246	38/7.11.64	H/10VRC	Must 11.15.65
William O. Quinn	6.324	23/7.8.65	2/MVCav	Never joined regiment

NAME	MSS vol. p	AGE/ MUSTER IN DATE	UNIT	SERVICE HISTORY
George Reynolds	1.699	24/9.7.61	C/10	Wnd 5.64. Trans 6.20.64 to
	3.824		Unass/37	Dis 9.10.64
Harvey L. Rhood	4.611	22/10.11.62	H/52	Dis for disab 4.30.63, Baton Rouge
William C. Rodman	1.624	23/8.18.63	A/9	Wnd 5.12.64, Spottsylvania, VA.
	3.465		B/32	Trans 6.10.64. Must 6.29.65
Joseph Root	6.174	19/12.23.63	F/1 MVCav	Must 6.26.65
Charles L. Russell	4.608	24/10.11. 62	G/52	Must 8.14.63
Frederick S. Russell	2.635	21/8.5.61	H/21	Wnd 9.1.62, Chantilly, VA. D of wounds 10.4.62, Douglas Hospital<, Alexandria, VA
H. Clement Russell	3.801	18/8.30.62	F/37	Wnd 5.5.64, Wilderness, VA. Must 6.12.65
John F. Russell	3.149	22/10.14.61	D/27	Sgt 3.23.63. Wnd 6.2.64, Cold Harbor, VA. D 6.4.64
Warren E. Russell	3.128	19/2.20.64	A/27	Pris 5.16.64, Drury's Bluff, VA. D 7.15.64, Andersonville, GA
Willard A. Russell	3.149	23/10.14.61	D/27	Invalid Corps, 9.18.63<. Trans 9.18.63 to F/10. Must 10.14.64
Jacob L. Rust	3.149	31/10.21. 61	D/27	Wnd 6.3.64, Cold Harbor, VA. Must 10.20.64

NAME	MSS vol. p	AGE/ MUSTER IN DATE	UNIT	SERVICE HISTORY
John Sammon	7.27	22/7.7.64	G/3 USlnf	Enlisted 22/7.7.64. Deserted 9.13.64
John Scannell (Scannal on plaque)	1.679	25/8.21. 63	K/9	Wnd 5.12.64, Spotsylvania VA. No further record
Aaron Scott				
Rufus P. Scott	5.367	34/1. 4.64	2 Bat/ MVLA	Must 8. 11.65
Daniel Sculley				
Silas Sebean	5.368	32/1.4.64	2 Bat/ MVLA	Must 8.11. 65
Thomas H. Sheppard	6.605	34/9.27.62	I/NH Bat'n/1 NEVC	Pris 6.18.63, Middleburg, VA. Paroled. Deserted 2.28.64, NYC.
Hiram Shumway<	2.702	27/7.18.63	I/22	Drafted. Wnd 5.30.64, Bathesda Church, VA. D 6.29.64, Emery Hospital<, Washington
Edwin B. Smith res: Deerfield^	3.149	22/9.13.61	D/27	Dis for disab 4.7.63, Boston.
	6.215	24/1. 6.64	L/1 MVCav	Missing 6.17.63, Aldie, VA. Must out of G 6.26.65. Same man?
Frederick H. Smith	3.149	18/9.20.61	D/27	Wnd 6.2.64, Cold Harbor, VA. Must 9.27.64
George M[yron ~] Smith	4.611	21/10.11.62	H/52	D 8.10.63, Mound City Hospital, Cairo, IL.

NAME	MSS vol. p	AGE/ MUSTER IN DATE	UNIT	SERVICE HISTORY
James W. Smith	3.413		D/33	Not commissioned by Gov as Order # 331,
	3.610	25/9.11.62	F/37	1 Lt in C/31. Resigned 4.10.62. 1 Lt. Dis 7.28.63 by Special Order # 331, War
	3.802			Dept. (6)
Joseph F. Smith		19/8.30.62	D/27	Wnd in arm< 5.6.64, Wilderness, VA.
	3.149			Must 6.21. 65
Lucius D. Smith		19/9.20.61	F/37	Wnd 5.15.64, Drury's Bluff, Va.
	3.802		H/52	Must 9.27.64
Samuel D. Smith	4.611	26/8.30.62	F/37	Must 6.21. 65
Joseph O. Spear	3.802	42/10.11. 62		D of disease 7.17.63, Baton Rouge
Charles O. Squires		20/8.30.62		Wnd 5.6.64, Wilderness, VA. Dis for wounds 11.10.64, Washington
Anton Stern	6.419			Deserted on way to 3/MVC
Francis J. Stockbridge	3.802	18/8.30.62	F/37	Must 6.21. 65
	3.802	21/8.30.62	F/37	Cpl. Dis for disab, 2.22.63.
Sylvester L. Stockbridge	7.121			Drafted 7.18.63, Long Island, Boston Harbor. Must 1.-.64<

NAME	MSS vol. p	AGE/ MUSTER IN DATE	UNIT	SERVICE HISTORY
Charles A. Story	4.668	20/7.18.63	B/54	Cpl 2.27.64. Sgt 3.1.64. Must 8.20.65
William A. Story	4.668	26/12.2.63	B/54	Must 8.20.65
James Sullivan	3.167	30/9.26.61	G/27	D 3.14.62, Newbern, NC
John Sullivan<	6.168	19/9.18.61	E/1 MVCav	Wnd -.-.62 as Cpl. Dis for disab 10.20.62, Washington
Michael Talbot	3.142	18/3.21.64	C/27	Pris 3.8.65, South West Creek, NC. Exch 3.27.65. Must 6.26.65
John Taylor	1.816	24/3.31.64	unassigned /11	Deserted 4.9.64, Gallup's Island, Boston Harbor
William Taylor	3.143	40/1.7.65	C/27	Pris 3.8.65, South West Creek, NC. Exch 3.27.65. Must 6.26.65.
Lyman B. Thayer (7)	3.187	18/7.24.62	unassigned /27	Dis for disab 10.22.62.
Samuel. M. Thayer	3.802	31/8.30.62	F/37	Dis for disab 4.1.63, White Oak Church, VA
Moses Thessier	3.802	19/8.30.62	F/37	Wnd 5.5.64, Wilderness, VA. Must as Cpl 6.21.65
Ciliste Thibault (Silas Tebo - Rebellion Bk)	5.369	32/1.4.64	2Bat/ MVLA	Must 8.11.65
Benjamin A. Till	4.704	19/11.30.63	I/54	D of disease 4.9.64, Jacksonville, FL

NAME	MSS vol. p	AGE/ MUSTER IN DATE	UNIT	SERVICE HISTORY
Samuel C. Till	4.674	18/12.11.63	C/54	Must 8.20.65
John Tompkins (no 1st name on plaque)	6.534	27/7.18.64	K/5 MVCav	Deserted 11.7.64, Point Lookout, MD
Alvin Trim				
John W. Turner	5.46	25/1.26.65	K/58	Must 7.14.65
John Vail	1.14	19/5.25.61	K/2	Pris 8.9.62, Cedar Mountain, VA. Must 5.23.64
Alfred Van Horn	1.699	23/6.21.61	C/10	Dis for disab 12.31.62
Avery A. Ward	3.429	26/2.19.62	F/31	Reen 2.16.64. Must from D/31 9.9.65
Charles Warren	2.833	20/1.7.65	K/24	Deserted 12.17.65, Richmond, VA
George H. Webber	1.14	19/5.25.61	K/2	Reen 12.30.63 in D/2. Pris, paroled 3.10.65, Annapolis. Must 7.14.65 from D
Lewis W. West	3.15	26/9.20.61	D/27	Cpl 11.-.64<. Dis for disab 3.23.63
Francis P. Wheeler	3.802	21/8.30.62	F/37	Wnd 5.5.64, Wilderness, VA. Dis for wounds 5.6.65
Charles H. White	4.611	18/10.11.62	H/52	Must 8.14.63
Francis M. White	1.699	19/6.21.61	C/10	D 5.31.62, Fair Oaks, VA
Charles H. Wilbur	4.611	23/10.11.62	H/52	Must 8.14.63

NAME	MSS vol. p	AGE/ MUSTER IN DATE	UNIT	SERVICE HISTORY
Ebenezer F. Wiley	3.803	22/8.30.62	F/37	Wnd 8.21.64, Charles Town, WVA. Trans to Veteran Reserve Corps. 1.20.65. Must 8.26.65 as Sgt K/VRC
Asa Williams, Jr. (8)			A/13 IV	Orderly Sgt. 3 months.
George H. Williams	2.636	27/8.5.61 7.26.61<	H/21	4 Cpl. Dis for disab 5.30.64
Isaiah Williams (8)			A/13 IV	1 Lt. 3 months.
John Williams				
Lyman Williams (8)			A/13 IV	Pvt. 3 months.
Charles Woston	3.144	28/1. 7.65	C/27	Pris 3.8.65, South West Creek, NC. Exch. Must 6.26.65
Orion E. Writer	4.868	20/3.10.64	I/57	Wnd 5.6.64, Wilderness, VA. Deserted 11.26.64, Washington. Returned under President's proclamation 5.28.65. Must 7.30.65
Joseph Young	4.611	19/11.4.62	H/52	Must 8.14.63

Endnotes

1. *Daily Hampshire Gazette,* 19 January 1990: 12, 1-6; 5 June 1990: 12, 5-6. Here and below I give both the page and column number because it is sometimes hard to locate material on the crowded pages.

2. Frederick B. Wichman, letter to the author, 27 January 1991. In the author's possession.

3. For a more contemporary appraisal of Hooker's military career, see Stephen Sears, "Fighting Joe Hooker," In Marla R. Miller, ed., *Cultivating a Past: Essays on the History of Hadley, Massachusetts* (Amherst: University of Massachusetts Press, 2009) 250-70.

4. 1860 U.S. census (Washington: The National Archives, 1965) 54.

5. *Hampshire Gazette and Northampton Courier,* 8 May 1929: 10, 2-3.

6. *Hampshire Gazette,* 16 February 1863: 1, 5.

7. *Hampshire Gazette,* 4 October 1864: 1, 7.

8. *Hampshire Gazette,* 24 January 1865: 2, 7.

9. *Hampshire Gazette,* 7 February 1865: 2, 7.

10. *Record of Soldiers and Officers in the Military Service* ("The Rebellion Book"), Town Hall, Hadley, lists some of these occupations. Others may be found in the Adjutant General, compiler, *Massachusetts Soldiers, Sailors, and Marines in the Civil War*. 9 vols. (Norwood, MA: Norwood Press and Boston: Wright & Potter, 1931-1937).

11. For further details, see Tom Pelissier, "The French-Canadians of Hadley, Massachusetts. Why they Came and Why They Stayed" (Amherst, Belchertown, Florence, MA: Collective Copies, 2009). The author quotes significant lines from a poem printed shortly before the war that linked New England broom corn with soldiers: "The Broom-corn stands on the meadow lands, / Like an army still and solemn, / When it holds its breath as the leaden death / Pours fast from the foemans' column." Edward C. Porter delivered his poem as part of the bicentennial ceremonies. *Celebration of the Two Hundredth Anniversary of the Settlement of Hadley, Massachusetts, at Hadley, June 8, 1859* (Northampton: Bridgman & Childs, 1859) 68.

12. Morris Treadwell, *Diary of a Binghamton Boy in the 1860's* (Endicott, NY: Marjory Barnum Hinman, 1982).

13. Ken Burns, *The Civil War*, Part 1: 1861

14. *Hampshire Gazette,* 27 August 61: 3, 3. Alfred A. Roe, *The Tenth Regiment Massachusetts Volunteer Infantry 1861-1864* (Springfield, MA: Tenth Regiment Veteran Association, 1909) 392, claims J. Howard Jewett as the first volunteer but does not say whether "April 26, 1861" is his date of enlistment or mustering in. There are two dates for Williams, July or August 1861.

15. Plaque in Historical Room, Goodwin Memorial Library, Hadley.

16. Luis F. Emilio, *History of the Fifty-Fourth Regiment of Massachusetts Volunteer Infantry 1863-1865*. 2nd ed. (Boston: Boston Book, 1894) 348 (Charles Story, William Story), 353 (Samuel Till), 375 (Francis Jennings), 382 (Benjamin Till). A sixth black soldier from Hadley, Henry Barber, is listed in *MSS* 7.321.

17. The degree to which northern soldiers were motivated by antislavery sentiment has been controversial among historians of the Civil War. For the alternative argument that northern soldiers "plainly identified slavery as the root of the Civil War," see Chandra Manning, *What This Cruel War Was Over: Soldiers, Slavery, and the Civil War* (New York: Vintage, 2008). Also James M. McPherson, *For Cause and Comrades: Why Men Fought in the Civil War* (New York: Oxford University Press, 1998). Since this volume appeared a number of additional books have captured the perspective of northern, and even Massachusetts, men who went off to fight. Some titles here include Lawrence Kohl and Margaret Richard, eds., *Irish Green and Union Blue: The Civil War Letters of Peter Welsh, Color Sergeant, 28th Massachusetts* (Bronx, NY: Fordham University Press, 1986); John J. Hennessey, ed., *Fighting With the Eighteenth Massachusetts: The Civil War Memoir of Thomas H. Mann* (Baton Rouge: Louisiana State University Press, 2000); and William C. Harris, *In the Country of the Enemy: The Civil War Reports of a Massachusetts Corporal* (Gainesville: University Press of Florida, 1999). See also Joan E. Cashin, *The War Was You and Me: Civilians in the American Civil War* (Princeton: Princeton University Press, 2002).

18. Hadley Records, vol 4: Elections, Town Meetings, Militia Lists, Highways (3/30/1857-12/1/1882) 134. Currently preserved in the vault of the Hadley Town Hall.

19. H. Clement Russell, "Personal Experiences in the Civil War," "Abraham Lincoln," written "Feb'y, 1919" [30]. In the author's possession.

20. Bell Irvin Wiley, *The Life of Billy Yank: The Common Soldier of the Union* (Baton Rouge: Louisiana State University Press, 1978) 109. The following quotation is on the same page.

21. *Hampshire Gazette,* 24 February 1863: 1.2. Since this essay was written new scholarship has enriched and complicated our understanding of support for the abolition movement in Massachusetts. See, for instance, Bruce Laurie, *Beyond Garrison: Antislavery and Social Reform* (Cambridge:

Cambridge University Press, 2005); and Julie Roy Jeffrey, *The Great Silent Army of Abolitionism: Ordinary Women in the Antislavery Movement* (Chapel Hill: University of North Carolina Press, 1998).

22. *Hampshire Gazette,* 14 January 1862: 2, 5.

23. Treadwell, *Diary of a Binghamton Boy,* 82. Town meetings recorded in Hadley Records routinely discuss the bounty question.

24. *Hampshire Gazette,* 9 December 1862: 1, 2.

25. *Hampshire Gazette,* 27 August 1861: 3, 3.

26. *Hampshire Gazette,* 5 May 1863: 2, 4.

27. *Hampshire Gazette,* 15 October 1861: 1, 5.

28. Hadley Records 169. Reported in *Hampshire Gazette,* 29 July 1862: 3, 3.

29. *Hampshire Gazette,* 25 March 1862: 1, 6.

30. *Hampshire Gazette,* 30 December 1862 2, 8.

31. *Hampshire Gazette,* 4 February 1862: 3, 2.

32. *Hampshire Gazette,* 10 June 1862: 3, 2.

33. *Hampshire Gazette,* 1 July 1862: 1, 6.

34. *Hampshire Gazette,* 6 May 1862: 3, 3.

35. *Hampshire Gazette,* 19 August 1862: 1, 6.

36. *Hampshire Gazette,* 19 January 1864: 1, 6-8.

37. See the lists of new buildings in *Hampshire Gazette,* 28 July 1863: 4, 1 and 11 August 1863: 3, 7. "Capt. I. H. Williams ... has made his father, Asa Williams of North Hadley, a present of a new house, which is to be immediately built. It will cost $1200." *Hampshire Gazette,* 26 July 1864: 2, 6.

38. H. Clement Russell, "The Captain From Belle Isle" (typewritten memoir, c. 1910) 2. In the author's possession.

39. *Hampshire Gazette,* 28 October 1862: 1, 4.

40. *Hampshire Gazette,* 29 July 1862: 3, 3. Naturally, the father did not go, but his son Alfred did.

41. *Hampshire Gazette,* 15 July 1862: 2, 8.

42. *Hampshire Gazette,* 5 November 1861: 3, 2 describing the 27th in Springfield.

43. *Hampshire Gazette,* 17 September 1861: 2, 1: "All the posts of non-commissioned officers of the regiment and the 2nd lieutenancies are vacant and will be filled from among the recruits, thus offering a chance of promotion to those who enlist."

44. It is confusing to follow the different bounties offered at different times. The usual amount from Hadley was $100-150. (Hadley Records) By 1863, a man who reenlisted could earn $325 from the state. Officers earned more, sometimes over $400 (*Record of the Massachusetts Volunteers*). Literally waving a flag, an ad for volunteers appeared in the *Hampshire Gazette,* 24 November 1863: 3, 7. See page 8.

45. *Hampshire Gazette,* 25 November 1862: 2, 4 gives some sample salaries for soldiers from Hampshire county. Lieutenant Colonel, $198 per month; Assistant Surgeon, $121; Quartermaster Sergeant, Sergeant Major, Hospital Steward, all $21. Privates usually received $13 no matter what county they came from.

46. Wiley, *Billy Yank,* 37-9.

47. *Hampshire Gazette,* 6 August 1861: 2, 6.

48. *Hampshire Gazette,* 19 November 1861: 2, 4.

49. *Hampshire Gazette,* 6 August 1861: 2, 6.

50. *Hampshire Gazette,* 14 January 1862: 3, 3.

51. *Hampshire Gazette,* 19 July 1864: 2, 7.

52. *Hampshire Gazette,* 19 July 1864: 1, 4.

53. *Hampshire Gazette,* 26 May 1863: 1, 5.

54. *Hampshire Gazette,* 16 June 1863: 2, 4.

55. *Hampshire Gazette,* 19 May 1863: 4, 1.

56. *Hampshire Gazette,* 6 August 1861: 2, 6.

57. *Hampshire Gazette,* 15 April 1862: 2, 6.

58. *Hampshire Gazette,* 22 October 1929: 2, 6.

59. *Hampshire Gazette,* 16 February 1863: 1, 5.

60. *Hampshire Gazette,* 8 December 1863: 1, 8.

61. This information is from the handwritten eligibility lists and militia lists in the Hadley Records.

62. Wiley, *Billy Yank,* 99.

63. H. Clement Russell, "Personal Experiences in the Civil War," "Gettysburg," "written from memory March, 1918" [18]. In the author's possession.

64. For some reason, there are no eligibility lists for 1863 in the Town Records.

65. Hadley Records, 272.

66. Hadley Records, 275.

67. *Hampshire Gazette,* 28 June 1864: 3, 1.

68. *Hampshire Gazette,* 31 May 1864: 2, 3.

69. *Hampshire Gazette,* 9 August 1864: 2, 3.

70. *Hampshire Gazette,* 26 July 1864: 2, 6.

71. *Hampshire Gazette,* 20 December 1864: 2, 7; 27 December 1864: 3, 3; 17 January 1865: 2, 7.

72. *Hampshire Gazette,* 7 January 1862: 1, 2. This schedule from the 27th training near Pittsfield, Massachusetts, sounds just like another day for the 10th training near Washington (*Hampshire Gazette,* 11 February, 1862: 2, 7) and for the 52nd on active duty at Baton Rouge (*Hampshire Gazette,* 31 March 1863: 1, 2).

73. *Hampshire Gazette,* 4 February 1862: 2, 8.

74. *Hampshire Gazette,* 27 May 1862: 2, 8.

75. *Hampshire Gazette,* 31 May 1864: 1, 3.

76. *Hampshire Gazette,* 9 December 1862: 2, 6.

77. *Hampshire Gazette,* 15 September 1863: 1, 5.

78. Burns, *The Civil War,* Part 2: 1862.

79. *Hampshire Gazette,* 3 June 1862: 1, 3-4.

80. *Hampshire Gazette,* 27 May 1862: 2, 8.

81. *Hampshire Gazette,* 10 September 1861: 1, 2.

82. *Hampshire Gazette,* 8 October 1861: 1, 2.

83. *Hampshire Gazette,* 27 May 1862: 1, 2.

84. *Hampshire Gazette,* 19 May 1863: 4, 1.

85. *Hampshire Gazette,* 15 September 1863: 1, 2.

86. *Hampshire Gazette,* 7 June 1864: 1, 3.

87. *Hampshire Gazette,* 10 June 1862: 1, 3.

88. *Hampshire Gazette,* 2 May 1865: 1, 4.

89. *Hampshire Gazette,* 26 May 1863: 1, 5.

90. *Hampshire Gazette,* 26 May 1863: 1, 5.

91. *Hampshire Gazette,* 19 May 1863: 2, 4.

92. *Hampshire Gazette,* 10 March 1863: 1, 5.

93. *Hampshire Gazette,* 23 August 1864: 2, 7.

94. *Hampshire Gazette,* 29 October 1861: 1, 2. Also *MSS.*

95. Wiley, *Billy Yank,* 124.

96. Levi Stockbridge, letter to Francis J. Stockbridge, 22 May 1864. In the author's possession.

97. *Harper's Weekly* 6.288 (5 July 1862) 421; *Frank Leslie's Illustrated Weekly* 14.354 (12 July 1862) 241; *Harper's Weekly* 6.301 (4 October 1862) 629; *Harper's Weekly* 6.311 (13 December 1862) 785 [front cover, with four other generals]; *Harper's Weekly* 7.319 (7 February 1863) 93; *Harper's Weekly* 7.332 (9 May 1863) 296-97 [with staff officers]; *Harper's Weekly* 8.398 (18 August 1864) 513 [front cover, on horseback, being welcomed into camp]; *Harper's New Monthly Magazine* 31.185 (December 1865) 639-44.

98. Walter H. Hebert, *Fighting Joe Hooker* (Indianapolis and New York: Bobbs-Merrill, 1944) 20.

99. *Hampshire Gazette,* 6 September 1864: 1, 5.

100. Hebert, *Fighting Joe Hooker,* 20.

101. Hebert, *Fighting Joe Hooker,* 23.

102. Hebert, *Fighting Joe Hooker*, 296.

103. Wiley, *Billy Yank,* 83.

104. Wiley, *Billy Yank,* 83.

105. Russell, 7.

106. *Hampshire Gazette,* 14 August 1862: 3, 2.

107. Biographical facts from the following sources: John Dunbar, "Pawnees," *Missionary Herald* May 1835: 202; September 1835: 343-49; October 1835: 376-81; November 1835: 417-21. These letters plus journal entries are conveniently gathered in *The Dunbar-Allis Letters on the Pawnee,* ed. Waldo R. Wedel (New York and London: Garland, 1985). John Brown Dunbar, Special Collections, Amherst College, Amherst, MA; "The Pawnee Indians. Their History and Ethnology," *Magazine of American History* (April, 1880): 241-81; "The Pawnee Language." In George Bird Grinnell, *Pawnee Hero Stories and Folk Tales* (New York: Charles Scribner's Sons, 1893) 409-37. Mr. Ron Benson, Farmington Hills, MI, also sent me his family tree – he is John Brown Dunbar's great grand nephew. I thank him for the information.

108. *The White Man's Foot in Kansas* (Topeka: State Printing Office, 1908) 41.

109. "The Pawnee Indians: Their Habits and Customs." *Magazine of American History* 5 (November 1880) 321. Many events in Blake parallel incidents in the lives of the Dunbars. In the film, Dunbar explains to the bewildered commander of Fort Hays (Maury Chaykin) why he is happy to proceed even farther west: "I've always wanted to see the frontier--before it's gone." Later, a Pawnee raider almost kills him with a war club. Echoing the missionary father and teacher son, the fictional Dunbar admits after he talks to Kicking Bird (Graham Greene), the holy man, "Nothing I have been told about these people is correct." These similarities make me understand why Michael Blake inscribed a copy of his book: "For Eric--who discovered the real John Dunbar."

110. Tim Giago, and others, "They've Gotten It Right This Time." *Native Peoples* 4 (Winter 1991) 6-14.

111. Michael Blake, *Dances With Wolves* (New York: Ballantine, 1988) 21.

112. Michael Blake, interview, *The Larry King Show*, Mutual Broadcasting System, Los Angeles, 7 January 1991. I thank Mr. Benson for his generosity.

113. Michael Blake, note to the author, postmarked 29 January 1991.

114. John Mark Lamberton, Kansas State Historical Society, Topeka, Kansas, 19 February 1991. The Kansan was from Mound City, Kansas, mustered in K/12 Kansas Volunteer Infantry on 9.30.62 and mustered out 6.30.65. He was not a sergeant. Michael Blake honestly said in the note to me that he only "believed" that was his model's rank.

115. Parker: Benjamin Capps, *The Old West: The Indians* (New York: Time-Life, 1973) 189; Plummer: Rachel Plummer, *Narrative of the Capture and Subsequent Sufferings ... During a Captivity of Twenty-one Months Among the Comanche Indians* (Houston: Telegraph Power Press, 1839) 108-10.

116. A few works cite father, son or both as experts in Pawnee culture. Weltfish, Milner and Murie apparently assume the two were one person. George Weltfish, *The Lost Universe: Pawnee Life and Culture* (Lincoln and London: Nebraska University Press, 1965) 53-54; 56; 472. George F. Hyde. *The Pawnee Indians* (Norman: Oklahoma University Press, 1974): 19 references. Alexander Lesser. *The Pawnee Ghost Dance Hand Game. Ghost Dance Revival and Ethnic Identity* (Madison: Wisconsin University Press, 1978) 339. Clyde A. Milner, *With Good Intentions: Quaker Work among the Pawnees, Otos, and Omahas in the 1870s* (Lincoln and London: Nebraska University Press, 1989) 471, first published as *Smithsonian Contributions to Anthropology*, No. 27 (Washington, DC, 1981). Martha Royce Blaine. *The Pawnees: A Critical Bibliography* (Bloomington: Indiana University Press, 1981), and *Pawnee Passage: 1870-1875* (Norman: Oklahoma University Press, 1990) 72; 151-53; 258; 320.

117. See table Hadley Residents Born Outside Massachusetts, page 40.

118. *Hampshire Gazette,* 25 March 1862: 2, 6; 26 March 1861: 3, 2.

119. J. F. Moors, *The History of the Fifty-second Regiment M. V. M.* (Boston: George H. Ellis, 1893) xxxvii.

120. Roe, *Tenth Regiment,* 392-93.

121. Burns, *Civil War,* Part 9: 1865.

122. W. H. Beaman, "A Discourse Delivered in North Hadley, Mass., on the Day of the Annual State Thanksgiving, Nov. 24, 1853" (Northampton: Hopkins, Bridgman, 1854) 19.

123. W. H. Beaman, "Exercises at the Semi-Centennial of the Dedication of the Church Edifice in North Hadley, November 20, 1884" (Northampton: Gazette Printing, 1885) 18.

HADLEY

1659-2009

350
YEARS

www.ingramcontent.com/pod-product-compliance
Lightning Source LLC
Chambersburg PA
CBHW020921090426

42736CB00008B/731